The Peony

Alice Harding's

Peonies in the Little Garden
&
The Book of the Peony

Introduced and Updated by

Roy G. Klehm

SAGAPRESS / TIMBER PRESS
Portland, Oregon

Color photography by Roy G. Klehm

ISBN 0-88192-274-9
Printed in Hong Kong

SAGAPRESS, Inc. / TIMBER PRESS, Inc.
9999 S.W. Wilshire, Suite 124
Portland, Oregon 97225

Library of Congress Cataloging-in-Publication Data

Harding, Alice.
    [Peonies in the little garden.   Selections]
    The peony : Alice Harding's Peonies in the little garden & The
book of the peony / introduced and updated by Roy G. Klehm.
       p. cm.
    Selections from the author's Peonies in the little garden and The
peony.
    Includes bibliographical references (p.   ) and index.
    ISBN 0-88192-274-9
    1. Peonies. I. Klehm, Roy. II. Harding, Alice. Book of the
peony. Selections. 1993. III. Title.
SB413.P4H2625   1993
635.9'33111—dc20   92-32021
                                                    CIP

Contents

List of Color Plates

Foreword

S O I sat at last and rested, till my eye was caught by certain white objects farther along the hillside, that were clearly too big by far to be flowers. . . . Through the foaming shallows of the copse I plunged, and soon was holding my breath with growing excitement as I neared my goal, and it became more and more certain that I was setting eyes on Paeonia moutan as a wild plant. . . . Here in the brushwood it grew up tall and slender and straight, in two or three unbranching shoots, each one of which carried at the top, elegantly balancing, that single enormous blossom, waved and crimped into the boldest grace of line, of absolute pure white, with featherings of deepest maroon radiating at the base of the petals from the boss of golden fluff at the flower's heart. For a long time I remained in worship and returned downward at last in high contentment.

On the Eaves of the World
—Reginald Farrer, 1917

Indeed, the phrase "high contentment" so aptly describes the internal feeling one experiences when marvelous discoveries of nature's flowers are eased upon our life's sojourn. We are all exposed to a wondrous array of beautiful flowers waiting for our appreciation; but to be truly alive and alert, to absorb, experience and marvel, to continuously learn—this is a blessing that few people have. Alice Harding, in her time, was one such person. Her appreciation of the beautiful peony was her high contentment. Pertinent, apposite, interesting, historically significant—these are some of the adjectives which describe the present-day value of Alice Harding's volumes, *The Book of the Peony* and *Peonies in the Little Garden*.

Harding was born in Keene, New Hampshire, and educated by private tutors at home and abroad. She married Edward Harding of the well-known law firm of Campbell, Harding, Goodwin and Danforth of New York City. At Burnley Farm in Plainfield, New Jersey, Mrs. Harding brought together in her garden a world-renowned collection of herbaceous and tree peonies, narcissi, tulips, irises, poppies, hemerocallis, lilies and lilacs. These plant collections were noted for their excellent quality; the mediocre had no place in Alice Harding's garden. She continually developed collections of the rarest and best varieties of peonies, maintaining and propagating them in her personal garden. Mrs. Harding always believed in testing and evaluating the finest new peony varieties and deplored the use of old varieties of insignificant value.

A graceful and forceful writer, her books are as fascinating as a novel and as authoritative as an encyclopedia, a rare combination. Mrs. Harding's thorough familiarity with the peony was earned from long years of growing and observation in her own garden. Her experience, critical taste and lively writing style give the reader an insight to the best peony knowledge of that time.

The Book of the Peony (1917) was Mrs. Harding's first book and was for many years the only one on the subject in America. In order to bring her knowledge of the peony to a far greater public, she wrote in 1923 the much smaller *Peonies in the Little Garden*, at the request of the publishers of the Little Garden Series. This volume had few equals in horticultural literature in its able treatment of its subject and its simplicity of expression. Mrs. Harding wrote her "little book" for gardeners who have at their disposal but a small amount of ground. As her two books cover much of the same information, the most comprehensive elements from each have been selected and consolidated into this new edition, which retains the original British or American spellings. New color plates are included.

Alice Harding originated and introduced a number of peony, iris, poppy, hemerocallis, and lilac varieties. During her life she also gave many exceedingly generous prizes to plant societies both in America and Europe, including three cups to the Royal Horticultural Society in England for the best peonies exhibited in 1924, 1925 and 1926. Because she tended to be shy, Mrs. Harding never exhibited her own fine flowers but preferred to encourage others to display their blossoms by sponsoring these prestigious awards.

Throughout her life, Alice Harding actively engaged in giving peonies from her own collections to botanic gardens in England, Scotland, Austria,

Canada, Colombia, New Zealand, Australia, India and South Africa. When giving the roots of these newer, finer varieties to gardeners in foreign countries, she encouraged altitude experiments where the latitude present precluded successful peony culture because of warm winter temperatures.

Alice Harding's horticultural interest and work were highly recognized. A rose, an iris, two French hybrid lilacs, a tree peony and two herbaceous peonies were named for her and in her honor during the 1920s and 1930s. In France, an honorary membership in the Société Centrale d'Horticulture de Nancy was conferred upon her. She was acknowledged with the Gold Medal from the American Peony Society in 1928 for promoting interest in the peony by the publication of her two books. Other honors were

> From the French Government, the Rank of Chevalier de Mérite Agricole; promotion to rank of officer; Honorary Diploma from the Minister of Education.

> From the Société Nationale d'Horticulture de France, diplomas and medals for her two books, *Peonies in the Little Garden* and *Lilacs en Mon Jardin*.

> From the Société Centrale d'Horticulture de Nancy, a specially bound folio-size book *Les Jardins de France*; a special crystal vase embossed with her namesake lilac, 'Mrs. Edward Harding'.

> From the horticultural library at Nancy, the naming of the library, the "Bibliothèque Alice Harding."

Mrs. Harding's shyness and modesty are seen in her written acknowledgment for the Gold Medal from the American Peony Society: "When one has worked hard from the sheer joy of the work itself, and without thought of reward, the pleasure of unexpected guerdons is more than doubled."

After a general, thorough introduction to peony appreciation and mythology, and both ancient and modern history of the peony, *The Book of the Peony* divides its attention between herbaceous and tree peony topics. As is true today, herbaceous peonies were more widely grown than tree peonies in the early 1900s.

Mrs. Harding thoroughly discusses the various types of peony blooms and how to distinguish them by their floral characteristics. She focuses particularly on the species *Paeonia albiflora*. Taxonomists have now changed this species name to *P. lactiflora*. Today's *lactiflora*, with its many

varieties, is one of the most common commercially available. Example varieties include the old-time favorites such as Sarah Bernhardt, Reine Hortense and Festiva Maxima, or the more recent introductions like Raspberry Sundae (Plate 22), Moonstone and Bowl of Cream. Appendix C offers a modern version of her "Short List" of recommended fine peonies (all *lactiflora*).

Even though the sensation of fragrance is a matter of individual taste, Alice Harding was sure that there must be a host of flower-loving noses as perceptive as her own. Modern peonies have acquired more pleasing fragrance as well as increased beauty. Because pleasing fragrance was especially important to her, a "Short List" of modern fragrant peonies is included in Appendix C.

A selection of peonies for use as cut flowers naturally includes those of the most delicate coloring. Mrs. Harding was careful to note that the beauty of these varieties was soonest lost in the light of the late spring sun. Cutting the partially open blooms, and bringing them into the house early, protects these delicate hues and allows the blossoms to open and show their full perfection. Appendix C also includes a "Short List" of delicately beautiful modern peonies that are ideal for cutting.

Since *The Book of the Peony* and *Peonies in the Little Garden* were written, extensive intercrossing of the various peony species has resulted in a wide range of new peony hybrid varieties. The general term "hybrid" or "herbaceous hybrid" is used to designate these progeny types. By combining the gene pools of these unique and distinguished species and specific varieties, many more blossom color combinations, plant forms and extended bloom seasons have become common. Yellows, corals, salmons, orange-reds, black-reds and pastels are now readily available for gardeners to discover and enjoy. Appendix D is a "Short List" of recommended modern fine herbaceous hybrid peonies.

These hybrid peonies extend the peony bloom season greatly, especially extending the early spectrum. Many of them bloom before the bearded iris season or at least coincide with it. Herbaceous hybrids can also have a different style, color and texture in their foliage and plant characteristics. The varieties within the species *tenuifolia*, for example, are fine-lobed and cut or lace-leafed.

The palette and variety of peony choices have significantly increased since 1917. The American Peony Society has published an attractive checklist of peony variety introductions from 1976 to 1986. The book contains 374 new herbaceous peony varieties registered by 25 plant breeders, and

54 new tree peony varieties registered by seven breeders. This is a sure indication of the high level of interest and hybridizing activity by both amateurs and professionals in the United States.

Soil preparation before planting is also dealt with thoroughly by Mrs. Harding. While today's gardeners generally realize how *very* important this step is for successful peony growing, the following comments may be helpful.

Gardeners blessed with reasonably good, friable, well-drained soil are best advised to dig individual holes for their peony roots approximately twice as large as the actual root size. More extensive excavations are generally not needed unless the soil is compacted and therefore has lost the natural capillary pores necessary for water and air movement. Young, healthy peony root divisions will usually adapt well to their new locations. While the theory of Mrs. Harding's extensive trench excavations is correct, large peony borders are generally not common in today's landscapes. Peony plantings are now often blended with other interesting perennials, smaller flowering shrubs and dwarf conifers to help create all-year garden interest and excitement. Peonies can thrive in soil where peonies have grown previously. Soil can be made better with good preparation including loosening it and using proper amendments. Nutrients can be added to the soil to adjust its pH level, and compost or other organic matter can be incorporated to help its enrichment. Other ways to heal soil are by double digging the garden and improving its drainage.

Container growing of ornamental plants has become popular in the last few decades. Peonies are often sold as container plants during the spring and summer planting seasons. Properly handled, this can be an effective way of establishing new peonies in the garden where previously only fall planting of bare-root plants was possible. Healthy plants with well-developed root systems can be transferred from their containers and will successfully establish themselves in the garden.

The recommended depth of planting of bare-root peony divisions varies with the amount of winter cold and late spring heat a particular geographic area generally receives. The mid to colder zones of a country where peonies generally do well would follow the standard two-inch depth recommendation. The more temperate or warmer winter zones would follow a one-inch to ground-level planting depth. Shallower planting in warmer zones exposes the plants to more winter cooling and also prompts the plants to bloom earlier, avoiding the possibility of intense late spring heat. Remember, most peonies are a natural cold winter climate plant.

Garden sanitation and fall cleanup are indeed important to prevent peony disease. If diseases strike, it is reassuring to know that carefully applied modern fungicides can be a helpful tool. Caution—a careful reading of the label and proper application are key considerations for the use of any garden spray product. Today, most thinking gardeners are also aware of the environmental impact of the use of garden chemicals.

Alice Harding's history of the tree peony is indeed interesting and informative. One marvels at the years and years of Chinese and Japanese history surrounding these splendid plants. Since 1917, however, exciting developments have affected the cultivation of tree peonies in the United States. The late Professor A. P. Saunders of Hamilton College in Clinton, New York, hybridized and developed many worthwhile new hybrids by intercrossing the species *lutea* and *delavayi* with existing Japanese Moutan varieties. Lemon yellow and golden yellow tree peony varieties, whose flowers are held upright above their foliage, are now available. Ivory and pearl shaded blossoms, blended and suffused with purple and cream pink, also resulted from his extensive efforts. In later years, Professor Saunders passed his work on to Nassos Daphis and William Gratwick. Nassos is still actively hybridizing these new tree peony lines into the fourth, fifth and sixth generations. Other modern breeding activity is evidenced by the previously mentioned fifty-four tree peony registrations representing a decade of work by American breeders. New varieties are also being grown in France and Japan, where tree peony interest is at renewed heights. Today's gardeners can look forward to a future of interesting new tree peony developments in a wide range of colors, forms and shapes. Appendix E is a "Short List" of recommended fine tree peony varieties.

Who would ever imagine that the gene pools of woody tree peonies and herbaceous *lactiflora* peonies could ever be combined! Initial breeding experiments linking these different peony species and vascular system types were first performed by Mr. Toichi Itoh of Japan shortly after World War II. His four yellow introductions are now appearing in the connoisseur market. In his honor, these hybrids are referred to as Itoh (pronounced EE-toe) hybrid peonies. Active American breeders are now working diligently to expand this breakthrough in modern peony cultivation. These initial Itoh hybrid plants have woody root systems and herbaceous stem tops. Preliminary thinking and experience indicate that they should be given culture treatments similar to those of herbaceous peony types. If Mrs. Harding were alive today, one can be sure she would be at the Itoh hybrid peony

forefront collecting, planting and growing them with enthusiasm at her Burnley Farm. Appendix F is a "Short List" of named Itoh hybrid peonies.

With herbaceous and tree peony interest at an all-time high, and gardeners ever eager for good plant literature, it is appropriate that Mrs. Harding's work is being republished. Serious gardeners can combine these well-written books with their other present-day peony literature. The American Peony Society offers an array of corresponding information and services to further help interested cultivators pursue peony growing excellence.

In closing, here is a pleasurable sampling of Alice Harding's philosophy:

"Had I but four square feet of ground at my disposal, I would plant a peony in the corner and proceed to worship."

"People should realize how much pleasure comes from the growing of even half a dozen peony plants, or three, or two . . . or just one."

"For to plan, to continue, to work in one's garden is, after all, the greatest part of one's joy in it."

"This peony was a large plant and surely cheered its owner for years."

"Yes, it is good to have a garden and it is better still to work in it."

"No garden can really be too small to hold a peony."

"The sight of a blooming peony has an inescapable lure for me."

"As the horses never trot so fast as around the fire in the winter, so the peonies never bloom so large and perfectly as in one's vision of the season to come."

—Roy G. Klehm

The Little Garden and the Peony

D EAR to the heart of man is the intimate in his surroundings. The little garden offers opportunities for affectionate understanding between the gardener and his work, not always in the possession of the owner of a large estate. In such places the numerous necessary retainers seem to stand in the way, be they ever so kindly and self-effacing. For to plan, to contrive, to work in one's own garden, is, after all, the greatest part of one's joy in it.

It is winter as I write these words, but my mind flies forward to the spring, to those joyous days when I shall labor again in my garden with head and heart and hands. Then every thought and every effort shall be trained upon the task of the moment. But through my work shall pierce my enchanted senses: the sweet-smelling earth, the fragrant breeze, the exulting sunlight, will all insist upon an occasional pause that I may revel in a sheer surge of joy. The droll singing of a young robin whose changing voice is lifted in the apple tree will compel a space of rest for delighted laughter. Then to the full may I taste that "spiritual gusto which lends a savor to the meanest act of living," as Lytton Strachey has so keenly phrased it.

Yes—it is good to have a garden, and it is better still to work in it.

No garden can really be too small to hold a peony. Had I but four square feet of ground at my disposal, I would plant a peony in the centre and proceed to worship.

Happily there are few gardens of such restricted area, and the opportunities to possess this lovable flower are greater than would appear at first glance. By a "little garden" I mean one ranging in size from fifty by one hundred feet to one or two acres. Notes and articles upon the peony which appear from time to time in catalogues and magazines deal frequently with large collections. Owners of small gardens are often fearful of having insufficient room for this stately subject. I think that they do not realize how much pleasure comes from the possession of even half a dozen plants, or three, or two—or just one.

One of the most amazingly interesting little gardens which I have ever seen was literally eight by eight feet. It was the tiny front-door plot before a cottage in Shottery. We were walking back toward Stratford on Avon after a visit to Anne Hathaway's cottage. The yellow blooms of St. John's-wort caught my attention, and I stopped to examine the handkerchief of ground wherein it grew. The healthy striking foliage of tall bearded iris was plentiful, and in a corner there was a peony,—only one,—an officinalis, probably rubra plena, though the bloom had passed. It was a large plant and had surely cheered its owner for years.

The peony in another tiny garden—or, to be more exact, the wreck of one—comes to my mind.

In March of 1919 I had a wonderful opportunity to see the battle-fronts of Europe from Nancy to Ostend. A sadder, more appalling vision of destruction never was. Town after town was leveled to heaps of brick and dust; tree after tree was deliberately sawed off and left to rot. The grapevines were pulled up, the fruit trees girdled, the land itself so shattered and upheaved that the gardener's first query was whether it could again bear crops before the lapse of many years.

We had left Amiens one Sunday morning, and passing Villers-Bretoneaux—where the Australian troops and some American engineers had made the stand that saved Amiens and the Western line—had gone through Hamelet, Hamel, Bayonvillers, Harbonnières, and Crepy Wood to Vauvillers. As the only woman in the party, I had been unanimously appointed in charge of the commissariat. It was noon when we reached Vauvillers. I chose a broken wall about fifty feet from the road as a good place on which to spread our luncheon. The car was stopped, the luncheon things were unpacked, and we picked our way over the mangled ground to the fragment of wall. As I passed around the end I came upon two peony plants pushing through the earth. Tears brimmed. I could not control them. Here had been a home and a cherished garden. As I stood gazing at the little red spears just breaking through the ground, a voice, apparently from the sky, inquired whether Madame would like a chair. Looking along the wall I saw the head of an old peasant woman thrust through a tiny opening. She smiled and withdrew, appearing a moment later with a chair. It was her only chair. She then brought forth her only cup and saucer, her only pitcher filled with milk, and offered us her only hospitality!

Joined now by her venerable husband, we listened to their story. The hiding of their few treasures, the burial of their bit of linen, their flight toward Paris, the description of the outrageous condition of the one room left for them to return to, made us burn with indignation. It was in her little

garden that the peonies grew. The fruit trees and shrubs were gone, the neat garden walls were blasted into space, the many precious flowers were utterly destroyed. When she found that Madame, too, loved *les belles pivoines*, she urged me to take one of the only two roots she had left!

We went away leaving the old couple laden with supplies, and I gathered from every man in our party a heavy toll of tobacco for a farewell gift of comfort. I hope she has again a little garden, with all the peonies that it will hold.

The sight of a peony has an inescapable lure for me. Quite unconsciously I pause on my way, and hang over any garden fence that encloses one. I suppose that if the fences were of high boards, still I should try to glimpse the peonies within, and seeking a convenient knot-hole, perhaps ruin my more or less perfect profile by pressing close to see!

In a little garden of half an acre or less were originated a few of the finest peonies of to-day. I refer to the garden of John Richardson in Dorchester, Massachusetts. That garden, so small but now so famous, was the expression of good taste. Richardson insisted on having the finest variety of every kind of plant he grew. Inferior things he rigorously discarded. The list of hardy perennials which had his love and care cannot in many instances be improved to-day. He applied a high standard of selection to the peonies which he produced from seeds. The influence of that little garden is beyond computation. Very clearly has it set an ideal toward which all other little gardens may well strive.

In the fall of 1922, Winnipeg, Canada, made a concerted effort to beautify the city. It adopted the peony as its civic flower, and started a campaign to plant a peony in every garden and yard. Professor Broderick writes me that the effort met with splendid success, and that thousands of roots were planted. No bit of land was too insignificant to do its share toward the permanent embellishment of the town.

These are but a few examples of the fitness of planting something long-lived in every little garden.

The peony is appearing more often, not only in our gardens, but in books. I have read lately of several heroines whose cheeks "mantled" or "blushed" or "burned" like a peony. It always used to be like a rose. When a flower once enters into the literature of a people, it may be safely held to be a part of that nation.

The fleur-de-lis, the rose, the thistle, the acacia have become national symbols. In a time not far away perhaps the peony will connote America, with a plant in every garden, big and little, and a place in every heart.

CHAPTER ONE

An Appreciation of the Peony

"Full of set flowers,
Full is my chamber;
Thou art most stately,
White peony."
—*Hakku.*

T HE peony[1] of to-day—too little known and too seldom sung—the brilliant result of years of steadfast devotion and untiring effort on the part of peony lovers and hybridisers, is the most superb and commanding flower which the garden holds. The iris, Oriental poppy, foxglove, hollyhock, lily, dahlia and chrysanthemum each has its own special radiance, yet each is surpassed by the peony with its magnificence of mass and perfection of detail. The rose, fine, exquisite and fragrant as it is, must yield first rank to the modern peony, which by reason of its sheer wealth of splendour and majesty of presence is now entitled to be called the Queen of Flowers.

The compelling charm of the improved types of peony lies not only in their grace and comeliness, but in the infinite variety of both flowers and foliage. Starting with single blooms, like huge anemones, through semi-double flowers, resembling water-lilies, and various enchanting forms of doubling up to the solid mass of petals, as in Avalanche, the peony holds one spell-bound in admiration. The wide diversity of foliage and habit of growth makes the plants an object of alluring interest. The leaves of certain sorts of peony are much divided and fern-like; of others, broad and strong with leathery quality. Usually varnished and lustrous, they run in colour range through many shades of green—often tinged with copper or with red. Some kinds are dwarf and bushy; some of medium height and spread-

---

1. I have adopted the spelling generally used in this country and approved by the Century Dictionary. In England "pæony" is the customary spelling. The botanical name is Pæonia.

ing growth, and others tall with a bold outline. All, however, have an air of sturdy character and self-reliance.

Fondly as I esteem the rose—heretofore the accepted standard of loveliness—I feel that the peony has the advantage over it, not only in superiority of flowers, but in other important points. The peony has no thorns to surprise or cause dismay. After the peony blooms its foliage remains an adornment—a contrast to the small and scanty leaves of the rose, which are often disfigured and unsightly. All through the garden season the peony has a landscape value which the rose lacks. And, last but not least, the peony requires neither spraying nor pruning: to the conscientious owner, burdened with the numberless details of spring garden-keeping, this is a welcome relief.

Fifty years ago the word peony meant one thing: it referred to the red "piney" of unfragrant memory, which, though highly prized and desirable at that date, suffers when compared with the beauties of to-day. Now the word peony conjures up a large variety of shapely flowers packed with glossy silken petals in a hundred shades, tints, and combinations of white, pink, yellow and red. One who sees for the first time typical specimens of the modern peony is thrilled with their breath-taking loveliness: even those who know well all the fascinations of the flower are stirred by it to new wonder and delight each recurring year.

Lest I be thought too loud in my praises of the peony, I will quote from one of many enthusiastic authorities—a book, too, which is not essentially a horticultural work. No one, I venture, will consider the Encyclopædia Britannica given to exaggeration in its statements, yet this is what it says about the peony:

"PÆONY (botanically Pæonia; Nat. ord. Ranunculaceæ q. v.), a genus of plants remarkable for their large and gorgeous flowers. There are two distinct sorts, one of the strong-growing herbaceous kind, with fleshy roots and annual stems, derived mainly from Pæonia albiflora and P. officinalis; the other, called the tree peony, stiff-growing plants with half-woody permanent stems, which have sprung from the Chinese P. moutan.

"The herbaceous pæonies usually grow from 2 to 3 ft. in height, and have large, much-divided leaves, and ample flowers of varied and attractive colors, and of a globular form in the double varieties, which are those most prized in gardens. They usually blossom in May and June, and as ornaments for large beds in pleasure grounds, and for the front parts of shrubberies, few flowers equal them in gorgeous effect. . . .

"The older varieties of P. albiflora include candida, Humei, Whitleyi, etc.; those of P. officinalis embrace albicans, anemoniflora, sabini, etc. The garden varieties of

modern times are, however, still more beautiful, the flowers being in many instances delicately tinted with more than one color, such as buff with bronzy centre, carmine with yellowish centre, rose with orange centre, white tinted with rose, etc. . . .

"The moutans, or tree pæonies, are remarkable for their sub-shrubby habit, forming vigorous plants sometimes attaining a height of 6 to 8 ft., and producing in May, magnificent flowers which vary in color from white to lilac, purple magenta, violet and rose. . . ."

Even had one never seen the flower, such fervour from a mere encyclopædia would awaken instant interest.

For those who as yet know the peony only in a general way, I will set out in orderly array no less than seven distinct and excellent reasons for considering the peony the best of all perennials:

1. **The sightly appearance of its blooms**

   The elegance of the flower, its different forms, the satiny texture of the petals and the numerous tints and shades of white, pink and red make its fairness a never-ending joy.

   In many kinds there is also found fragrance equal to that of the rose.

2. **Its worth for both landscape and cutting**

   Both in mass and in detail, it answers many requirements. The substantial size of the plant and of the individual flowers makes it a useful and striking subject for the garden architect. The brightness, sweetness and lasting qualities of the blooms make it an ideal cut flower.

3. **The freshness of its foliage throughout the summer**

   A number of perennials lose the freshness of their foliage after blooming and have to be cut back or hidden by other plants. Except in one or two instances, the shining foliage of the peony attracts attention from the time of its appearance above ground until it succumbs to the late frosts.

4. **The ease of its culture**

   Any one can raise peonies successfully with far less trouble than it takes to grow roses.

5. **Its practical freedom from insects and disease**

   While a number of diseases of the peony have been classified and described, the grower who reads and heeds directions is not likely to be troubled with diseased plants.

6. **Its extreme hardiness**

It thrives in very severe climates, and endures a degree of cold that is fatal to many other perennials.

7. **Its permanence**

Lifting and dividing the roots are not necessary for at least eight or ten years. Many varieties can be left undisturbed for fifteen years or more.

The peony has but two drawbacks—which can hardly be considered objections. (1) It increases slowly. (2) The stems of some varieties are not strong enough to bear the weight of the large flowers and must be supported.

As far back as 1629, peonies were so well liked and so much planted in gardens that John Parkinson in his quaint book on plants, "Paradisi in Sole, Paradisus Terrestris, or a Choice Garden of all Sorts of Rarest Flowers," gives descriptions of six different kinds with four interesting pictures. Referring to "Pæonia femina vulgaris flore plena rubra," which closely resembles and in all probability was P. officinalis, he says: "This double peony, as well as the former single (Pæonia femina Byzantina—the single red Peony of Constantinople) *is so frequent in every garden of note, through every country,* that it is almost labour in vaine to describe it: but yet because I use not to pass over any plant so lightly I will set down the description briefly in regard it is so common." A little further along he breaks through his scholarly reserve with true horticultural ardour, and expresses his real regard for the peony by exclaiming, "no flower that I know so faire, great and double." I wish that it were possible for Parkinson to see the peonies of to-day, but I doubt if he could phrase his admiration any more charmingly than he did for the less wonderful peony of 1629.

As the horses never trot so fast as around the fire in the Winter, so the peonies never bloom so large and perfectly as in one's vision of the season to come. After one's appreciation of and enthusiasm for the peony are fully awakened, there is not a week in the year when the flower is not a pleasure. At all times, night or day, Winter or Summer, one can in absorbing study be amongst the peonies and in imagination behold them again in all their sumptuousness.

When the Spring is here at last, and the earth has its indescribable scent of warmth and sweetness, I hasten to my peony garden to see if the first coral tips have broken through the ground. After a few days, becoming impatient, I loosen the soil and dig quietly and gently, until I find the little

red points that will soon grow into sharp red spears. Then, reassured that they are really coming, in spite of the long time Winter has held them on the way, I cover them up and go away content. On that day, for me, the garden season begins.

I know of no plant that is so satisfyingly beautiful in every stage of its development. The changing of the shades of red, green, copper and bronze of the young stems and foliage, the slow unfolding of the leaves of fine design are exquisite in themselves—and yet they are but a prelude to the burst of glory in the flowers. When the blossoms appear, it is indeed hard to leave the garden: no matter how many times a day one gazes at them, there is something newly entrancing on each successive glance. There is one peony lover, bewitched by their spell, who, loath to leave them for even a few hours, makes the rounds of her garden every night with a lantern. This mistress of a much-cherished garden often rises to listen to the birds and see her peonies at dawn. The piercing tenderness of the woodthrush's song, the dream-like purity of the peonies, the inspiration of the summer morning, bring a happiness that is poignant, a thankfulness for life that is ecstasy itself.

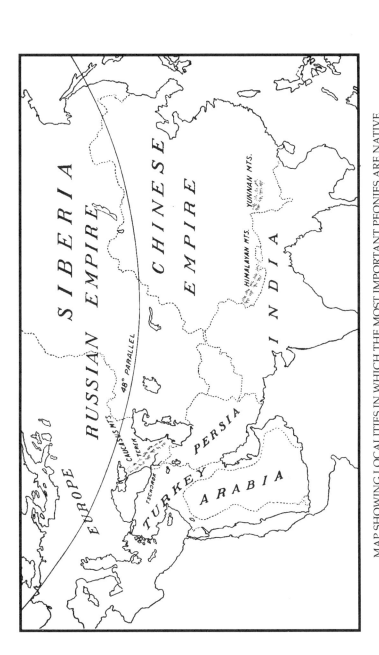

MAP SHOWING LOCALITIES IN WHICH THE MOST IMPORTANT PEONIES ARE NATIVE

P. Albiflora: Central China and Siberia. (There is no exact   P. Lutea: Yunnan Mountains, Southern China.
information as to just how far north P. Albiflora grows.)   P. Moutan: Central part of Western China.
P. Emodi: Himalayan Mountains, India.   P. Officinalis: Europe, south of 48th parallel.

Note: The only peony native to America is P. Brownii, which is found in California and the Northwest.

CHAPTER TWO

The Mythology, and Ancient and Modern History of the Peony

THE peony has been such a familiar flower in humble gardens in this country that many persons are not aware of its aristocratic and extended genealogy. The descent of the peony can be traced through numerous periods of history even into mythology; indeed in Greece, the Roman Empire, China, Japan, France, England and America, its relation to mankind has been considerable.

In medicine, art, commerce and science, the peony has played a part which not only entitles it to general recognition, but which is also absorbing in detail. At different times in the past, it has been the object of many journeys and voyages, the subject of years of painstaking study, and to its improvement men have lovingly devoted a large portion of their lives. From Leto, mother of Apollo, who appears to have been the original "introducer" of the peony, down to M. Dessert, the great French grower, who in 1915 sent out his latest peony under the name of "Victoire de la Marne," we have a long and entertaining story, of both horticultural and human interest.

For greater convenience and clearness I have set out in tabular form some of the facts one should have in mind in order to read without confusion the complete history of the "peony"—which generic name includes several species, each with a separate record.

TABULATION OF PRINCIPAL SPECIES OF PEONIES

I. **Herbaceous Peonies**

These are bushy plants two to four and one-half feet high that die down to the ground in the Autumn. When the word "peonies" is used reference generally is made to herbaceous peonies (in distinction to tree peonies).

1. P. OFFICINALIS (*of the apothecaries' offices or shops — used for medicinal purposes*)—

the red single or double peony of old-fashioned gardens. White single and double varieties have also been known for over three hundred years.

This species is a native of southern Europe and is the peony of mythology and of Greek and Latin literature. It is grown to some extent in gardens now. This species gave the genus its name.

2. P. ALBIFLORA (*white flowered*)—Improved type—with red, pink, white, mauve or yellowish flowers of several forms, single, semi-double, crown, bomb, rose, etc., and many of them fragrant. This is the most important and interesting species of the herbaceous group and is the principal one grown to-day. It is sometimes called P. sinensis or Chinese peony.

The primitive type of P. albiflora—from its name, presumably white—is a native of a vast range of territory from the central regions of Siberia to central China. Its early history is entirely in China and Japan: it was not known in Europe prior to 1656.

The improved type was obtained:

   (a) By importation into Europe from Siberia or China about 1850.

   (b) By crossing P. albiflora (either the imported primitive type or the imported improved type) and certain little-known species, *e.g.*, P. peregrina (*foreign*), P. arietina (*ram's horn fruited*), etc.

   (c) By crossing P. albiflora (either the imported primitive type or the imported improved type) and P. officinalis. This crossing, done chiefly since 1850, is probably the origin of most of the beautiful double kinds of to-day with their varied forms and exquisite colourings.

3. P. TENUIFOLIA (*narrow-leaved*)—introduced into England in 1765 from the Caucasus.

4. P. WITTMANIANA (*Wittman's*)—A pale yellow peony. Discovered in the Caucasus about 1842. One of the parents of the desirable Wittmaniana hybrids.

5. P. EMODI (*Mt. Emodus*), the only peony native to India.

6. P. ANOMALA (*unusual*), P. CORALLINA (*coral red—referring to the seeds*), P. DECORA (*comely*), P. PEREGRINA (*foreign*), P. BROWNII (*Brown's*)—the only peony native to America—and others, are less important species from a gardening standpoint.[1]

II. Tree Peonies

These have woody stems that do not die down to the ground in the Autumn. They have been much cultivated in China and Japan for many centuries.

1. P. SUFFRUTICOSA (*woody*) or P. MOUTAN—with large flowers (eight to ten inches across), of various shades of red, white, pink, salmon and purple.

---

1. A list of these is given in Chapter 10.

A native of the central part of western China, it was first exported to Japan in 724; and first exported to England (and thence to France and the United States) in 1787.

2. P. LUTEA (*yellow*). Discovered in southern China in 1882. The main portion of this book is devoted to herbaceous peonies. Two chapters (8 and 9) cover tree peonies exclusively—their description, history, planting, cultivation, propagation and best varieties.

THE PEONY IN MYTHOLOGY AND IN THE CLASSICS

Zeus and Leto were the parents of Apollo, god of healing, who was the father of Æsculapius, god of medicine. According to the ancient writers, Pæon, pupil of Æsculapius and physician of the gods, first received the peony on Mt. Olympus from the hands of Leto. With it he cured Pluto of a wound inflicted by Hercules during the Trojan war. To quote from Homer's Iliad with its stirring action: "Pluto also endured a swift shaft when the same hero (Hercules) the son of Ægis-bearing Jove, afflicted him with pains at Pylos amongst the dead. But he went to the palace of Jove on lofty Olympus, grieving in his heart and transfixed with pain; for the shaft had pierced into his huge shoulder and tortured his soul. But Pæon healed him, applying pain-assuaging remedies."[2]

This cure caused so much envy in the breast of Æsculapius that he secretly plotted the death of Pæon: probably the first recorded instance of professional jealousy. But the wicked plotter was destined to be foiled. Pluto, in gratitude for what Pæon had done, saved the physician from the fate of mortals by changing him into the plant that had been used in the cure. This plant has ever since borne Pæon's name.[3]

The history of the cognate word pæan is interesting as showing some of the possibilities of etymology. After the time of Homer, the name of healer and the office of healing were transferred from Pæon to Apollo, who was thenceforth invoked by the cry "Io Pæan" (ΠΙ ὡαιάν) sometimes made to him as physician and at other times made to him irrespective of his healing art. Subsequently, a pæan was a choral song to Apollo or Artemis, his twin-sister (the burden being "Io Pæan"), in thanksgiving for deliverance

---

2. Iliad, 5, 401, etc. Another apparent instance of the peony's efficacy as a cure for wounds is also given in the Iliad (5, 899, etc.). "So spake he (Jove) and bade Pæon heal him (Mars). And Pæon laid assuaging drugs upon the wounds and healed him seeing he was in no wise of mortal mould. Even as fig juice rapidly thickens white milk that is liquid before but curdleth while one stirreth it, even so swiftly healed he impetuous Mars."

3. The Latin name Pæonia is the feminine of Pæonius—"belonging to Pæon."

from evil. Later it was addressed to other gods on similar occasions,[4] and then to mortals. Now it is a "loud and joyous song": witness this book.

The peony was known to Greek writers under the name pæonia and also under the name glucuside—"having sugar qualities"—evidently referring to the honey secretion of the flower buds. It is mentioned in the works of a number of early authors, among whom are Pliny, Theophrastus, Dioscorides and Galen.

Pliny, in his Natural History (about 77 A.D.) gives the first detailed description of a peony plant and seeds, but does not mention the flower. He says: "The plant known as pæonia is the most ancient of them all. It still retains the name of him who was the first to discover it, being known also as the 'pentorobus' (from its five seeds which resemble vetches), by some and the 'glucuside' by others. . . . It grows in umbrageous mountain localities and puts forth a stem amid the leaves, some four fingers in height, at the summit of which are four or five heads resembling Greek nuts in appearance; enclosed in which there is a considerable quantity of seed of a red or black colour. This plant is a preservative against delusions practised by the Fauni in sleep (nightmare). . . ."[5]

Pliny devotes one chapter to a fuller description of the plant and sets out twenty ills or diseases of the human body which it will cure. Among these are jaundice, gnawing pains in the stomach and certain affections of the trachea. He says it acts as an astringent and then adds: "It is eaten also by beasts of burden, but when wanted for remedial purposes four drachmæ are sufficient."[6]

Dioscorides, a medical man who flourished in the first century of the Christian Era, describes about five hundred plants in his Materia Medica. The peony is included in this work. The famous Viennese Manuscript of Dioscorides, painted and written in Byzantium for the Princess Anicia Juliana in the early part of the Sixth Century, contains a number of brush drawings of plants and flowers, some of which closely resemble our specimens of to-day. Unfortunately, the illustrations of the two peonies mentioned in the text—Pæonia arren [P. corallina] and Pæonia theleia [P. officinalis] are missing. The lifelike representation of his favourite flower was evidently too great a temptation for some peony lover to resist.

---

4. Liddell & Scott, Greek-English Lexicon (1888), p. 1106.
5. Natural History: Book 25, Ch. 10.
6. Natural History: Book 25, Ch. 60.

HERBACEOUS PEONY HISTORY IN CHINA AND JAPAN

In China and Japan the popularity of the herbaceous peony was somewhat overshadowed by that of the tree peony, but the former kind has long had a distinct recognition in both countries. In China it was called "Sho Yo" meaning "most beautiful," which bespoke a considerable appreciation on its own account, even though the tree peony was ranked as the King of Flowers. It served as a sort of Forget-me-not which one friend bestowed upon another on separation. A Sho Yo plant was also presented for a friendly remembrance after separation. These customs are referred to in a Chinese song:

> "If anyone will give his friend a present
> He hands a gift 'most beautiful' of all."

In 536, A.D., the herbaceous peony was fairly well distributed over the country and was used for medicinal purposes and in a number of places even for food for human beings. The appreciation of its dietary value was another instance of the advanced character of the civilisation of China, for the peony as a source of nourishment was surely but the prototype of some of our modern breakfast foods. Hung King writing at this time, distinguished two sorts, the red and the white, which is the first mention we find anywhere of a white peony.

In 968, Mas Ze, an author on natural history and natural philosophy, discoursed learnedly at considerable length on the herbaceous peony. In the early part of the Eleventh Century, according to another Chinese historian of the period, the herbaceous peony was grown in all parts of China but the most valuable roots came from the district of Huni Gan Foo—wherever that was.

By 1086, as a literary botanist of that date tells us, gardeners realised the possibilities of the plant for ornamental purposes and began, by the application of strong fertilisers and great diligence in cultivation, to produce flowers of large size. As a result of these efforts and the extensive propagation by planting of seeds, new and better varieties were produced. In 1596, more than thirty improved kinds were listed in the catalogues of Chinese growers.

As to the subsequent history in China not much information is readily accessible. Loureiro in 1790 says that P. officinalis was grown over the entire Chinese Empire, but principally in the northern provinces, and that it had been imported to Cochin China. In the middle of the Nineteenth Cen-

tury, a number of valuable peonies were shipped to France and formed the foundation of collections made by noted French amateurs. At the present time, while the peony is still grown extensively, few exportations to Europe or this country are made—due possibly to the quality of Chinese varieties as compared with the improved varieties of this side of the world, or else to the lack of initiative of the Chinese in distributing their horticultural products.[7]

Among the number of beautiful things for which Japan is indebted to China, few equal the peony. Early in the Eighth Century, the Japanese imported from China both the herbaceous and the tree peony. The herbaceous peony was called "Skakuyaku"—apparently a corruption of the Chinese Sho Yo—and has been highly thought of, although not accorded the honours given the tree peony, which is ranked as one of the three Royal Flowers.

In Japanese literature and folklore the peony is the subject of many poems and stories. It is not clear in each case from the translation whether the herbaceous or the tree peony is referred to, but it is evident that both kinds were cherished in the hearts of this flower-loving people. There is a little Japanese verse that shows that East and West meet in the kindred pleasures of the garden if nowhere else:

> "When Spring is on the wane,
> Then men are apt
> To turn their thoughts
> To peonies again."

At the present time, there are several nurseries in Japan which grow both herbaceous and tree peonies. One of these, which does a large export business to England and America, maintains an office in each country. Twenty-nine varieties of the herbaceous peony are listed in the catalogue of this nursery, the names of some of which are delightfully quaint. Someganoko—painted fawn, Shishi-Odori—dancing lions, Kame-no-Kegoromo—turtle's holiday attire, are among the most diverting. The present exportations from Japan of herbaceous peonies consist principally of a form of peonies of a distinct type known as the Japanese, which constitutes a separate class intermediate between the single and double types.

---

7. At the present time (1916) inasmuch as the Chinese Government has not complied with the regulations of the United States Department of Agriculture as to inspection, peonies cannot be imported from China to this country.

IN ENGLAND

The knowledge of flowers and plants in Saxon times (about 477–1017) and for several subsequent centuries, was chiefly based on the works of Pliny and Dioscorides. These two authors were largely drawn on by Apuleius, who lived about 150 A.D. His Herbarius, written in Latin, was later translated into Anglo-Saxon, and must have been one of the horticultural "best sellers" of the day, as there are no less than four MSS. extant.

Alexander Necham, born in 1157, was an early English writer on gardening. After some years spent as a student and professor in Paris, he became the abbot of the Augustine monks at Cirencester. In those days monasteries had gardens of considerable size and the monks "went in heavily" for raising herbs, vegetables and flowers. In Necham's De Naturis Rerum, he gives a description of what a "noble garden" should contain. "The garden," he writes, "should be adorned with roses and lillies, turnsole, violets and mandrake; there you should have . . . fennel, coriander . . . and peonies." It would seem that all these plants were cultivated in typical gardens of the time. The peony of this date was in all probability P. officinalis.

In the Fourteenth Century peonies were used for seasoning. In Langland's Vision of Piers Plowman—a popular allegorical poem, written about 1375—a priest asks a poor woman:

"'Hast thou ought in thy purs', quod he
'Any hote spices?'
'I have peper and piones' (peonies) quod she,'
        and a pounde garlike,
'A ferthyngworth of fenel seed, for fastyng dayes.'"

In another poem of the same century, entitled "The Pearl," the flowers around an arbour are described:

"I entered in that arber grene
In augeoste in a high seysoun
    *   *   *   *   *   *
Shadowed this wortes ful schyre (bright) and schere
Gilofre (clove-pinks) gingure (tansy) and
        groomylyon (gromwell)
And pyonys powdered ay betwene."

It thus appears that at this early day the use of the peony in the hardy border had begun.

In 1484, about 300 years after Necham, the Herbarius credited to Arnol-

PIONIA

❡Pionia calida & ſicca in ſecundo gradu. Cuius ra⸗
dix in medicinis ponitur cum reperitur in receptis
eligenda eſt illa quæ nigra exiſtit continua non per
forata.& in hyeme colligitur & per annum ſeruaṫ.
Virtutem habet occultam contra epilentiam & ſu⸗
ſpenſam collo præſeruat ab epilentia:teſtante Galie
no experto de quodaȝ puero cuius collo talis radix
appéſa erat & non patiebaṫ:radice.n.ſubtracta ſta⸗

PAGE FROM HERBARIUS OF ARNOLDUS DE VILLANOVA, PUBLISHED IN 1484.

This is the first known printed picture of the peony.

dus de Villanova was published on the Continent. This book contains probably the first printed picture of the peony—a wood-cut in which flowers, leaves and roots are completely conventionalised (see illustration, page 18). In addition to its historical interest, the quaint stiffness of the wood-cut has a charm of its own. The text, which is in terrific mediæval Latin, is mainly devoted to the use of the peony for medical purposes, and is based on Galen. Later English writers made use of this work freely.

In Tudor times (1485–1603), contemporary authors mention peonies together with other old favourites—jasmine, lavender, lilies, rosemary, rocket and snapdragon—as being grown in the knottes or beds that were then coming into fashion.

The many names under which the peony was known in England indicate that the flower was widely grown and was regarded with affection. Some of these names were: chesses, hundred-bladed rose, marmaritin, piny, pie nanny, nan pie, pianet, piano rose, posy, sheep shearing rose, rose royale.

In 1597 John Gerard, a physician and practical gardener of Holloway, near London, published his Herbal. In this book, which was founded on A History of Plants by Dodoëns, a Hollander (1554), four pages are devoted to peonies and eight illustrations are given. The text and pictures are so engaging that I have reproduced one of the pages (see illustration, page 20). Gerard speaks of the medicinal virtues of peonies: "The black graines (the seeds) to the number of fifteen take in wine or mead . . . is a special remedy for those that are troubled in the night with the disease known as Ephialtes or night mare which is as though a heavy burthen were laid upon them, and they oppressed therewith, as if they were overcome by their enemies or overprest with some great weight; and they are also good against melancholick dreams."

In "The Taming of the Shrew" (1603), Shakespeare refers to peonies in the line: "Thy banks with peonied and lilied brims."

In 1629, John Parkinson, King's herbarist, apothecary and traveller, who possessed an excellent garden near London, published his "Paradisi in Sole, Paradisus Terrestris" (a play on his name, Park-in-Sun's Earthly Paradise) "or a Choice Garden of all sorts of Rarest Flowers with their Nature, place of Birth, time of flowering, Names of Vertues to each plant, useful in Physick or Admired for Beauty." In this book, after describing six kinds of peonies—two of which were double—Parkinson says, "All these Peonies have been sent or brought from divers parts beyond the Seas; they are endenizened in our gardens where we cherish them for the beauty and

4 There is found another fort of the double Peionie not differing from the precedent in ftalkes, leaues,or rootes: this plant bringeth foorth white flowers wherein confifteth the difference.

3 *Pæonia fœmina multiplex.*
Double red Peionie.

4 *Pæonia fœmina polyanthos flore alba.*
The double white Peionie.

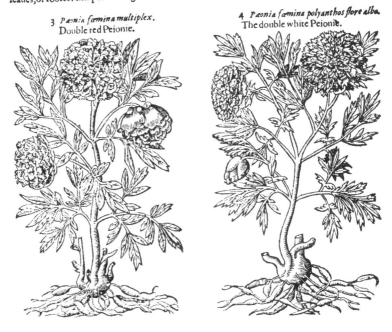

There is another kinde of Peionie (called of *Dodonæus Pæonia fœmina altera,* but of *Pena Pæonia Promifcua feu neutra*: in Englifh Maiden or Virgine Peionie) that is like vnto the common female Peionie,fauing that his leaues and flowers are much fmaller , and the ftalkes fhorter , and beareth red flowers,and feede alfo like the former.

We haue likewife in our London gardens another fort bearing flowers of a pale whitifh colour, very fingle,refembling the female wilde Peionie,in other refpeƈts like the double white Peionie.

※ *The place.*

All the forts of Peionies do grow in our London gardens,except that double Peionie with white flowers,which we do expeƈt from the lowe countries of Flaunders.

The male Peionie groweth wilde vpon a conie berrie in Betfome, being in the parifh of South-fleete in Kent,two miles from Grauefend, and in the grounde fometimes belonging to a Farmer there called *Iohn Bradley.*

※ *The time.*

They flower in May,the feede is ripe in Iuly.

※ *The names.*

The Peionie is called in Greeke παιονία: in Latine alfo *Pæonia,* and *Dulcifida* :in fhops *Pionia*: in high Dutch Peonien blumen: in low Dutch Maft bloemen: in French *Pinoine*: in Spanifh *Rofa del monte*: in Englifh Peionie: it hath alfo many baftarde names, as *Rofa fatuina,Herba Cafta,* of fome *Lunaris,*or *Lunaria Pæonra*: bicaufe it cureth thofe that haue the falling ficknes, whom moft men do call *Lunaticos,* or Lunaticke. It is called *Idæus Daƈylus*: which agreeth with the female Peionie,

delight of their goodly flowers as well as for their physical vertues." Of the two double peonies described by Parkinson, one was white and one red. It has been suggested that the double white had originated as a sport of the double red.

The first Botanical Garden in England was established at Oxford by the Earl of Danby, about 1621 "for a nursery for simples." In this garden, as appears by the catalogue, there were "double and single Peony" in company with twenty kinds of roses, including York and Lancaster. In the History of Plants at Oxford by Robert Morrison (1620–1683), who was noted for being one of the pioneers in the systematic botanical classification of plants, there is a description of several peonies including a flesh-coloured peony.

In the well-known Botanists' and Gardeners' Directory of Philip Miller, Keeper of the Chelsea Botanic Garden of the Worshipful Company of Apothecaries, which work first appeared in 1731, seven kinds of peonies are set out as all the sorts the author had observed in English gardens. The seven are two varieties of corallina (both single), officinalis (single, large double and small double), a double white and Lusitanica or Portugal peony. Of the last variety Miller says: "The Flowers of this kind are single, but do smell very sweet which renders it worthy of a Place in every good Garden." It is difficult to identify this variety with certainty at the present time although it is probably Broteri.

During the latter half of the Eighteenth Century several additional kinds, including tenuifolia, peregrina and anomala, were cultivated in England.

In the early part of the Nineteenth Century some varieties of albiflora were imported from China that are still offered by growers. Among these are Fragrans (Sir Joseph Banks, 1805), Whitleyi (Whitley, 1808)—which the importer had been led to believe was a yellow tree peony—and Humei (Anderson, 1810). Fragrans was the earliest sweet scented double variety grown in England.

In 1837, the variety Pottsii was described as the most splendid of the five albifloras cultivated in English gardens. It had been introduced from China by John Potts—an intrepid plant-collector—in 1822, and named after him.

The first large collection of named peonies in England was made by Loddige in Hackney in 1845, and was sold eight years later. In 1850, Salter, a nurseryman, began a collection with the albifloras, Edulis superba (splendid, with edible roots), originated by Lemon in France in 1824, Pottsii and Reevesii, and some other varieties imported from Belgium. In

his catalogue, of 1855, twenty-four double sorts are listed. At this time, peonies began to have such a large sale that Salter was unable to supply the demand for P. Grandiflora nivea plena (double large snow white)—originated by Lemon in 1824—P. lutea plenissima (very double, yellow)—originated by Buyck in Belgium in 1842—and several of the others that he offered.

In addition to the above-named varieties, the first hybridisers in England had three forms of P. officinalis—rubra (red—the common double red), rosea (rose) and carnescens plena (double flesh white)—with which to make a beginning.

In 1864, James Kelway, of Somersetshire, made his first attempt in improving existing types. He commenced in a modest way with P. officinalis and P. corallina, but soon went into the growing of peonies on a very extensive scale. Twenty years later he catalogued two hundred and fifty varieties of which sixty-three were new single and forty-one new double varieties of his own raising. Through his energy in introducing and distributing improved forms Kelway did much to make the peony popular in England. Among his best productions are Baroness Schroeder (1889), Miss Salway (1905) and Kelway's Glorious (1909).

Peter Barr was a tireless collector of all species of the peony and was also much interested in hybridising. From his establishment have come Wittmaniana rosea, one of the Wittmaniana hybrids, and the albifloras, Helene Leslie, Lord Rosebery and Celestine.

In 1885, a First Class Certificate of the Royal Horticultural Society was granted to a peony named Snowflake—the first peony to receive this honour.

About 1890, after a period of many years, during which exotics and bedding plants were in great demand, the newer and better varieties of peony brought that flower into prominence again. The successful work of French growers who devoted much time to hybridising the peony was largely responsible for the revival of its fashion. Since then the peony has gone forward rapidly both in improvement and popularity.

At the Royal Gardens at Kew and Glasnevin and at Chiswick, there are large collections of peonies for the enjoyment and education of the public. At the Royal Horticultural Society's Gardens at Wisley, a comparative trial, held about 1896, is now (1916) being repeated with the newest forms raised since then. The reports will be published in the Journal of the Society.

In France

The history of the peony in England is chiefly the history of its cultivation in gardens from the earliest time. In France the record of the improvement of the individual flower in recent years is the main thing that has come down to us. There is an account of one famous peony, P. daurica (brought from Siberia via England), which was introduced about 1810 as a rare plant at Malmaison for the Empress Josephine.[8]

France has given the world the most numerous and famous growers and hybridisers of the peony, whose efforts during the past century produced many of the finest varieties we see in the best collections at the present time. The work of improving the peony was begun earlier in France than in England and soon became of great interest to royal and aristocratic connoisseurs. Among the varieties we have to-day were some originated between 1830 and 1848 in the garden of King Louis Philippe at Neuilly under the care of his gardener, M. Jacques.

Before this, probably the first man in Europe to raise peonies from seeds and to offer the best of these as named sorts was M. Lemon of the Porte St. Denis, Paris. As far back as 1824 (about the time when hybrid perpetual roses began to be popular), he raised a lot of seedlings of P. officinalis from which came P. anemoniflora alba and P. grandiflora nivea plena. The last named of these—white, shaded with salmon,—though one of the oldest hybrids, even now ranks among the best. In the same year, P. edulis superba—a peony still much grown—was also produced by Lemon. In 1830, he originated P. sulphurea—white, tinted yellowish green—a kind sufficiently attractive to be cultivated to-day. Lemon achieved not only greatly desired modifications in colour and form, but also a pleasing fragrance which exists in most of his varieties and is very marked in some of them.

Modeste Guerin, starting in 1835, in Paris, with plants brought from China and Japan, made rapid advances in improving the peony. From then until 1866, he introduced more than forty new varieties: among them General Bertrand (1845), Modeste Guerin (1845), Duchesse d'Orleans (1846), Dr. Bretonneau (1850), Madame de Vatry (1853) and Alexandre Dumas (1862), are conspicuous for their excellence. It is interesting to note that Guerin succeeded in getting in several of his peonies a touch of yellow, which up to this time was almost an unknown colour in this flower. Some of his varieties that had yellow in them were put out before the first yellow peony—P. Wittmaniana—was discovered. Three instances of what he ac-

---

8. For a full account of this peony see Description des Plantes Rares Cultivées a Malmaison et Navarre. A. Bonpland, Paris, 1813. This species is also known as P. corallina, var. triternata.

complished in this regard are Grandiflora lutescens (1840), with fleshy white guard petals and a yellow centre, Reine des Français (1842), with fleshy pink guard petals and white centre shaded yellow, and Triomphe de Paris (1850), white with yellowish centre. Guerin also produced some red peonies—chiefly with magenta tints—which owed their dark colour to P. Pottsii.

By 1840, the Prince de Salm Dyck, an amateur horticulturist who was a native of Cologne but who resided for many years in Paris, had imported a number of valuable plants direct from the Orient. These apparently passed to the House of Solange Bodin near Paris. From 1845 on, some fine new double varieties were sent out by this establishment: none of these, however, are capable of identification at the present time.

The collection raised by M. Jacques was inherited by his nephew, M. Victor Verdier, presumably after the revolution of 1848 and the dethronement of Louis Philippe. Verdier had produced some new varieties prior to this date, but sixteen of his best kinds—still offered by growers to-day—were put out between 1855 and 1861. One of Verdier's most noted peonies is the incomparable Marie Jacquin.

Comte de Cussy was an enthusiastic amateur who started with importations from China and raised from them a number of distinctive varieties. It was from his large collection in other hands that a very high development of the peony was subsequently reached. About 1850, M. Calot, of Douai, acquired the collection of the Comte. From then until 1872, with rare imagination and diligence he originated over twenty new kinds, many of which are greatly prized in gardens now. Among them are Philomele (1861), Solfatare (1861)—until the introduction of Primevere, the nearest approach in a hybrid to a yellow peony; the exquisite Duchesse de Nemours (1856), Madame Lemonier (1860), Eugenie Verdier (1864), Madame Crousse (1866), Couronne d'Or (1872), La Tulipe (1872), Monsieur Dupont (1872).

In 1872 the collection of J. Calot passed into the hands of M. Crousse, of Nancy, who continued to send out selections from the Calot seedlings until 1879 and who later, from 1882 to 1898, introduced a large number (over seventy-five) of seedlings of his own. Under Crousse the peony was bred up to such a point that it seems almost impossible to improve upon his work. The name Crousse attached to any peony can always be taken as indicating merit. Among the varieties of Crousse are: Modele de Perfection (1875), Livingstone (1879), Madame Emile Galle (1881), Felix Crousse (1881), Madame de Galhau (1883), Madame de Verneville (1885), Ava-

lanche (1886), Asa Gray (1886), Mademoiselle Rousseau (1888), Monsieur Jules Elie (1888), Marguerite Gerard (1892).

Contemporary with Guerin, Verdier, Calot and Crousse was Etienne Mechin, an ardent amateur who, tutored by the celebrated horticulturist, Bretonneau, began to collect peonies as early as 1840. By 1860, he had acquired a famous collection comprising importations from China and Japan, and seedlings of his own raising. Madame Ducel (1880) and Raphael (1882)—a valuable early red—are two of his best products. With his grandson, Auguste Dessert, Mechin put out a number of new sorts among which were Adolphe Rousseau (1890) and Suzanne Dessert (1890). Mechin was succeeded by Dessert who has added many noteworthy varieties and is still actively engaged in this work at Chanonceaux. Dessert is considered one of the greatest living experts on peonies. He has produced Madame D. Treyeran (1889), Marcelle Dessert (1899), Monsieur Martin Cahuzac (1899), Germaine Bigot (1902), Aurore (1904). The Mechin-Dessert group is one of the most important in the history of the peony in France.

Within the past twenty years, Victor Lemoine of Nancy, who occupies the old establishment of Crousse,[9] has become one of the world's greatest hybridisers in peonies as well as in other plants. His varieties—the most recent of the French introductions—are notable for their distinction of form and colouring in addition to their rare beauty. Among the best of his productions are La Fiancée (1898), Madame Emile Lemoine (1899), Alsace-Lorraine (1906), Sarah Bernhardt (1906), Le Cygne (1907), Primevere (1907), Lamartine (1908).

Other names closely identified with the development of the peony in France are Miellez (who originated Festiva Maxima [1851]), Pele, Delache, Gombault, Foulard, Seneclauze, Paillet, Millet, Brochet and Croux.

---

9. Tabulation showing successive owners of noted French collections of peonies:
   1. Etienne Mechin (1815–1895), collection started 1840
      Dessert and Mechin, 1882–1893
      Auguste Dessert, 1888–, now extant at Chanonceaux
   2. Comte de Cussy
      Calot, 1850–1872
      Crousse, 1875–1898
      Victor Lemoine, 1898–, now extant at Nancy
   3. M. Jacques, gardener to Louis Philippe, 1830–1848
      Victor Verdier, 1848–1866
      Eugene Verdier, 1866– ?
      Part of this collection was acquired by Dessert.
   4. Modeste Guerin, 1835–1866
      A large part of this collection was bought by Mechin. The ground in Paris occupied by this collection and by that of Eugene Verdier was sold for building purposes, and the collections were dispersed.

IN AMERICA

The fact that the peony does not appear in horticultural literature in this country before 1800 may be accounted for more by the absence of the literature than the absence of the peony. Not till the beginning of the Nineteenth Century did horticulture as distinct from agriculture attain some individuality. The literature arose with the art.

Bernard McMahon in his American Gardeners' Chronicle—an ambitious work published in 1806—gives a list of perennials suited to the open ground in the Middle and Eastern States. He includes five kinds of peonies: "P. officinalis: common peony; albiflora: white flowered peony; laciniata: jagged-leaved peony; hybrida: mule peony, and tenuifolia: slender-leaved peony." Presumably all these existed in America when the book was printed, although it has been cruelly suggested by one critic that McMahon's lists were compiled from English sources.

As might be expected, the peony appears in the Catalogue of John Bartram & Son of their "Foreign Plants Collected from Various Parts of the Globe" and cultivated at their Botanic Garden at Kingsessing, near Philadelphia (1807). The reference, as in all cases in the catalogue, is merely the name—"Pæonia officinalis"—without description or comment. In the Catalogue of Bartram's Garden published in 1828 (five years after John Bartram's death), we find six herbaceous peonies in addition to some tree peonies:

"Pæonia officinalis	crimson officinal pæony		.25
" albicans	double white	"	.25
" rosea	rose coloured	"	.25
" rubra	double red	"	.25
" carnescens	flesh coloured	"	1.00
" albiflora simplex	single white	"	1.00"

In Green's Treatise on Ornamental Flowers, published in Boston in 1828, peonies are included among the "leading plants" of the day. And in the same year there is a record of the elder Thomas Hogg exhibiting a single white P. officinalis at an exhibition of the New York Horticultural Society.

William Prince, of Flushing, Long Island, in 1829, in his annual Catalog of Trees and Plants cultivated at his famous Linnæan Botanic Garden, says: "No class of flowers has recently attracted more attention in Europe than the peonies. . . . Most of the varieties are extremely splendid and others possess striking peculiarities. Anticipating that a similar taste would

be evinced in this country, the proprietor has, by a great exertion, obtained every variety possible from Europe and also a number from China." He lists forty kinds containing a great diversity of shades and colours. The prices range from fifty cents to twenty dollars, but most of the plants are quoted under two dollars.

An elaborate botanical work published in 1846–1850—The American Flora, by Dr. A. B. Strong—contains coloured plates and descriptions of P. officinalis, P. peregrina, P. edulis Reevesiana and P. Russi, all of varying degrees of red and magenta. I say "of varying degrees" advisedly: the plates were coloured by hand and I am credibly informed no two of them were alike!

The introduction of a number of varieties of the species of P. albiflora, which occurred about 1850, caused an increase in the popularity of the peony in this country. The merits of this type—fragrance, great hardiness, erect habit of growth, variability as to colour and form of flowers—all combined to create a demand for this new "Chinese peony," the name by which it began to be called. As reproduction by division of the roots was extremely slow on account of the limited quantity of the several kinds, propagation by seeds was resorted to. Cross pollination, either accidental or directed by hybridisers, in time gave rise to scores of novel forms of flowers.

In 1858, H. A. Terry of Crescent, Iowa, one of the pioneers among peony experts of this country, obtained from William Robert Prince, who had inherited the Linnæan Botanic Garden, at Flushing, thirty varieties of P. albiflora, including Humei, Pottsii, Reevesii, Comte de Paris, fragrans, festiva maxima, lutetiana, edulis superba, plenissima rosea and Queen Victoria. Many of these freely produced seeds from which Terry soon had thousands of seedlings growing. He selected the best for further propagation but found that generally not five—often not one—in a thousand were worth cultivating. During a long life time—longevity and peony growing seem to go hand in hand—Terry produced over a hundred new varieties among which are a few very beautiful ones—Stephania, Grover Cleveland, dark crimson, and Mrs. McKinley. Shortly before his death, Terry sold most of his collection for twenty-five hundred dollars.

John Richardson, an enthusiastic lover of ornamental plants, raised in his small garden in Dorchester, Massachusetts, a number of important new varieties of peony. Some fragrant flowers of his growing are noted as far back as 1857, about thirty years after the first fragrant peonies were produced in France. From that year until his death in 1887 he was actively

engaged in growing seedlings. He had only a few mature plants—some forty albiflora peonies—but in addition he carefully tended their descendants, "candidates for fame" as he called them. He originated about eighteen double varieties distinguished by their fine form, colour, vigorous upright habit, large size and uniformly high quality. Many of them were awarded certificates of merit by the Massachusetts Horticultural Society. The chief stock from which his seedlings came probably was: Festiva Maxima, Festiva and Pottsii plena, and a double white seedling originated by Mr. Carter of the Harvard Botanic Garden.

A good example of Richardson's work is Walter Faxon, conspicuous for its pure and beautiful rose-colour. Others are Milton Hill, another of the finest pink peonies, Perfection, Dorchester, Charles Sedgwick Minot and Grandiflora. Most of his varieties are light in colour and late flowering. Richardson's seedlings were not offered for sale until after his death, at which time all of his productions were named by his friends, John C. Hovey and Prof. Robert Tracy Jackson, of Cambridge, Massachusetts.

Richardson's success in producing new varieties of great worth and beauty is an inspiration. He showed how even a small garden may prove large enough to bring enduring fame to its devoted owner.

George Hollis, of South Weymouth, Massachusetts, during the "nineties" originated about one hundred new varieties. All of his productions are very scarce and many high-priced at the present time. Among the best are Standard Bearer (1906), Adelaide E. Hollis (1907), George Hollis (1907), Loveliness (1907) and Maud L. Richardson, which is among the tallest peonies, often growing five feet high.

T. C. Thurlow, of West Newbury, Massachusetts, was one of the early growers in this country. Starting in 1875, after some years' work he got together a large collection which included most of the varieties which had been introduced. James Hartshorn of Chicago, on looking over Mr. Thurlow's grounds, examining the labels and taking note of the different kinds, asked that a price be named for the whole lot of peonies. On all of his peonies, except two plants each of a hundred varieties, Mr. Thurlow fixed nine thousand dollars, which figure was forthwith accepted. The collection filled two freight cars. After the plants had been shipped, Mr. Thurlow started to get up a new collection, better than the one he had sold.

Recently the seedlings of Brand—notably Martha Bulloch (1907), and Frances Willard (1907)—have aroused much admiration. The beautiful productions of Shaylor, among which are Frances Shaylor (1909), Jessie Shaylor (1909), and Mary Woodbury Shaylor (1910), show what is being

accomplished in this country by careful hand pollination.

Other persons who, as hybridisers or growers, have been closely connected with peony history in this country since 1850 are: Mrs. Sarah E. Pleas, now over eighty-five years of age, who originated Jubilee and Opal No. 2, Rosenfield (Floral Treasure, 1900, and Karl Rosenfield, 1908), Fewkes, Ellwanger, Peterson, Ward, Barry and Harrison.

The admiration in this country for the peony, which started about 1850, has continued to wax—with occasional wanings—until the present time. But the growth in favour has had disadvantages as well as advantages: about 1900, the number of different varieties introduced from seeds and from importations of plants (chiefly from England and the Continent) had grown to such a size that considerable confusion in nomenclature was caused. The difficulty a purchaser had in getting the kind ordered became so great that it seriously affected the peony trade as well as the dispositions of many peony buyers. Unscrupulous growers—some, alas, are always with us—put on the market hundreds of new seedlings which they christened with good old names. One expert feelingly described the condition of the peony business at this time as "utterly chaotic."

To replace confusion with order a few peony enthusiasts and growers in the summer of 1902 started the movement which resulted in the following year in the incorporation of the American Peony Society, of which C. W. Ward was the first President, and A. H. Fewkes the first Secretary. The original purpose of the Society was "to advance public interest in the peony and especially to straighten out peony nomenclature." In 1904, the Society agreed to co-operate with the Horticultural Department of the Experiment Station at Cornell University for the purpose of making a study of all the varieties of peonies which it was possible to obtain. To an appeal for plants of different kinds, a liberal response was made by those having large collections. Nearly every prominent grower in this country sent samples from his stock: in addition contributions were made from the finest collections in Europe, including two hundred plants from A. Dessert at Chanonceaux.

The first plantings at Cornell in 1904 soon increased to thousands of specimens having upwards of twenty-six hundred names—practically all the varieties in commerce. Within three or four years most of the plants were well established and had begun to yield characteristic blooms. For five years the Nomenclature Committee of the Society, Bertrand H. Farr and Joseph Dauphin, together with an expert horticulturist at Cornell, Dr. Leon C. Batchelor, worked over this collection and compared their obser-

vations with studies carried on by them at several of the large nurseries in the eastern part of the country. With painstaking and disinterested labour, nearly all distinct varieties usually grown were identified and described as to form, colour and fragrance of flower and vigour, habit and floriferous qualities of the plant. After eliminating the numerous synonyms and the kinds wrongly named—in a number of instances the same variety appeared under as many as twenty different designations—the twenty-six hundred names contained in the complete list were sifted down to five hundred separate meritorious varieties. These five hundred—which were mostly varieties of P. albiflora—comprise nearly all of the peonies of value to be found in the entire collection. The description in detail, a check list of peonies and numerous data in reference to the peony, have been published in four Bulletins by Cornell University, 1907–1911. The Peony Society has thus rendered a service of incalculable benefit to the peony growers not only in America, but everywhere. The amateur is thankful for its efforts whenever he places an order, or wants assistance in identifying some plant in his garden.

The American Peony Society has also done valuable work in other lines. It has held large and successful exhibitions at New York, Chicago, Philadelphia, Boston and Ithaca. The splendid display of flowers shown has attracted attention and aroused enthusiasm, which has rapidly increased in the past few years. In 1911, at the exhibition held in Philadelphia, the sum of two hundred and thirty-two dollars was offered in prizes. In 1916, at the New York exhibition the aggregate of the premium list was six hundred dollars, divided among twenty-six classes. At this exhibition there were over fifteen hundred blooms staged, and more than sixteen thousand persons attended. The American Peony Society has issued reports from time to time and has recently started the publication of a bulletin containing items and articles of interest in reference to the peony called "Bulletin of Peony News" which appears twice a year.

In 1916, The Northwestern Peony and Iris Society was formed in Minneapolis.

Best Varieties and Their Characteristics

HE selection of any flowers for the garden is largely a matter of taste and therefore an expression of personality. In order to make a choice, however, one must have a clear idea of existing varieties and which of these are obtainable. As we have seen, hundreds of varieties of P. albiflora have been listed; but as many have proved to be the same as others, with different names, and many are so inferior as to be not worth cultivating, the number of available kinds that are desirable is not so overwhelming as might at first appear. Broadly speaking there are about five hundred varieties which are admirable in gardens: this list of five hundred might advantageously be restricted to a much smaller number containing only those of distinction and value.

A MAIN LIST

I give a Main List of one hundred and twenty-five varieties selected on their merits. It includes desirable peonies of all prices, from a few of the new and costly seedlings down to some of the most charming of the inexpensive sorts. As several of the loveliest peonies fortunately increase with comparative rapidity they may be bought at reasonable prices: a number of attractive kinds may be purchased as low as fifty and seventy-five cents apiece. One of the delights of a peony garden is that it is possible to lay the foundation of a satisfying collection by starting with the standard varieties of moderate price, and adding the more rare and costly roots from time to time as one's experience and taste direct, and one's garden bank account permits.

SHORT LISTS

Immediately preceding the Main List will be found six Short Lists which are intended to assist those who are unacquainted with the different vari-

eties of peonies or whose preferences may be for white, or pink, or red peonies. In each of these colours, I have made a selection of kinds which are considered among the best. A list of peonies of distinction and beauty at a low cost, and another list of rare and exquisite peonies for the enthusiastic collector are added. These Short Lists are lettered A, B, C, D, E and F, and are referred to in column 4 of the Main List.

The varieties of P. albiflora which I give in the Main List, together with the species described in Chapter 4, are the most striking and beautiful peonies for our gardens. Species such as P. arietina, P. corallina, P. decora and others are best left for ardent collectors to study and experiment with: for while extremely interesting as members of the peony family and possibly useful for hybridisation, they lack size, charm and variety of colour. Although the herbaceous peonies of Japan have much merit and are well worth a place in our gardens, it is impossible to give an extended list of their names that would be dependable. As the peonies ordered from Japan seldom come true to description or even twice alike, the direct importation of these peonies must be undertaken as a pleasing game of chance. One or two growers in this country and in France have propagated from imported Japanese stock, and from these growers a few, but only a few, good ones can be obtained with assurance of getting what is ordered.

In preparing the Main List, which is intended to be a guide and not an exhaustive study of each flower, the descriptions have been made as simple and untechnical as is practical. Brief explanations as to a few botanical terms, "types," colours and fragrance will, nevertheless, be necessary.

TYPES

In the process of development from the original single type, the herbaceous peony has acquired certain forms or types which have been classified and named "bomb," "crown," "rose," etc., the full descriptions of which I set out below. The stamens—the fertilising organs of flowering plants, consisting of (a) filaments or supports, and (b) anthers or double sacs filled with pollen—have in some types of the peony broadened and thickened into additional petals called staminodes. Likewise the carpels— the seed-bearing organs—have developed into petals called carpelodes. For brevity and convenience staminodes and carpelodes are usually called petaloids. The words staminodes, carpelodes and petaloids are all used in describing types. When the word "guards" is employed it means the outside or primary petals. When the word "differentiated" occurs reference

is made to the degree of difference in appearance between the outside petals or guards and the petaloids within.

The names of the types and their descriptions follow:

DETAILS OF TYPES

1. SINGLE

Single

Peonies of this class are composed of a few broad petals, a single row of which surrounds a mass of pollen-bearing stamens and seed-bearing carpels.

Example: Le Printemps.

2. JAPANESE

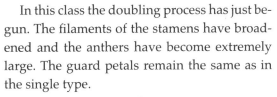

Japanese

In this class the doubling process has just begun. The filaments of the stamens have broadened and the anthers have become extremely large. The guard petals remain the same as in the single type.

Example: Mrs. McKinley.

3. ANEMONE

Anemone

This is the next development in the process of doubling. The filaments of the stamens are still broader than in the Japanese type, having become narrow petals which fill the centre of the bloom. While the anthers have completely disappeared, the centre petals are still narrow and short. There are few high-class varieties of this type.

Example: Anemoniflora rubra.

4. SEMI-DOUBLE

Semi-double

Flowers of this type contain filaments which have widened irregularly, making petaloids of varying widths throughout which stamens are mixed. The guard petals may or may not be clearly differentiated.

Example: Stephania.

Crown

5. CROWN

In this class the petaloids originating from the carpels differ from the petaloids, developing from the stamens as well as from the guard petals.

Example: Madame de Vatry.

Bomb

6. BOMB

In this type the petaloids derived from both carpels and stamens have become much broader, without any crown, but still are clearly differentiated from the guard petals.

Example: Felix Crousse.

Semi-rose

7. SEMI-ROSE

In flowers of this class all the petals are uniformly wide, differing from the full rose type in the presence of a few stamens.

Example: Asa Gray.

Rose

8. ROSE (FULL-DOUBLE)

This type completes the process of doubling. All the stamens and carpels have developed into petals resembling the guard petals.

Example: Mme. Lemonier.

PLATE 5. America (plant patent 4246). These pure fire-engine-red blossoms were named in honor of America's bicentennial.

PLATE 6. Angel Cheeks. A neat blend of pastels, creams and pinks that makes an excellent cut flower.

PLATE 7. Bridal Icing. A glistening, pure white flower.

PLATE 8. Cheddar Charm. A nicely contrasting blend of gold and white.

PLATE 9. Chiffon Parfait. Fluffy textured and of the softest pink color, with large blossoms.

PLATE 10. Companion of Serenity. Quite possibly the most beautiful and graceful soft pink tree peony, with refined blossoms of an attractive ruffled shape.

PLATE 11. Coral Charm (plant patent 4247). Rich coral-colored peony.

PLATE 12. Ivory Jewell. A classic flower form with rich ivory outer petal coloration.

PLATE 13. Kamada Fuji. Tree peony with large, flat double blossoms of a rich wisteria lavender.

PLATE 14. Leda. Tree peony displaying unusual lavender-pink blossoms with an underlay of alluring yellow.

PLATE 15. **Marchioness.** Tree peony displaying large tan and harvest gold blossoms with inner red flares.

PLATE 16. Moon River. An excellent double-blossom form of intriguing soft cream-pink.

PLATE 17. Persephone. Tree peony with soft yellow double blossoms that are excellent in form.

PLATE 18. Pillow Talk. A shell-pink, billowing flower that is very fragrant.

PLATE 19. Pink Hawaiian Coral. Attractive and alluring coral with a hint of rose, and a nice semidouble form.

PLATE 20. Pink Lemonade. A neat blend of pinks, pastels and creams that is very fragrant.

PLATE 21. Prairie Moon. Early blooming with a pleasant soft yellow color.

PLATE 22. Raspberry Sundae. So named for its vanilla ice cream dripping with raspberry topping.

PLATE 23. Salmon Chiffon. An inviting salmon pink with superb flower form.

PLATE 24. Spring Carnival. Tree peony of a pearled ivory, cream and pink blend with picotee-type edging.

PLATE 25. White Ivory. The classic Venus of white double peonies.

PLATE 26. Zephyrus. Tree peony with a rainbow of lavender, cream, beige and pink hues.

COLOURS

In the Main List, I have given in ordinary terms the details of shadings and combinations immediately under the name of each variety and have placed the colour of the general effect in a separate column. I have avoided the use of such expressions as Tyrian rose, Solferino red and purple-garnet (which as a matter of fact contains less purple than other shades bearing no mention of purple). The colour terminology used by the professional growers is confusing and misleading to a beginner. For the information of those who care to compare the trade terms with actual samples of colour, I would state that the chart used by the American Peony Society is the "Répertoire des Couleurs pour aider a la détermination des Couleurs des Fleurs, des Feuillages et des Fruits." This elaborate work, published by the Société Française des Chrysanthèmistes in Lyons in 1905, comes in three volumes, or rather portfolios, and contains over fourteen hundred shades. There has been some discussion as to the respective merits of this chart and Ridgeway's "Colour Standards and Nomenclature."[1] Much is to be said in favour of each chart. However, as there are many garden owners who do not possess either, or do not feel the need of one, I have not employed the cryptic colour terms used in both.

It is to be noted that the colours of all peonies vary somewhat in accordance with the age and strength of the plants and the constituents of the soil. There may be an intensification of colours in different years due to the vagaries of the weather. This year, 1916, Avalanche had such a strong tinge of yellow throughout as to appear almost another flower. Allowance should also be made for the fact that peonies fade in strong sunlight.

SIZE AND SEASON

Size is also a comparative matter. The actual dimensions in inches vary in each case with the degree of cultivation. The descriptions, "very large," "large," "medium" and "small," which I have used in column 6, refer to the size of the peony in question compared to other varieties of peonies grown under the same conditions.

The different varieties of albiflora have a season of bloom which lasts from three to four weeks. Reference to their comparative time of bloom within this season is made in column 7. In the vicinity of New York the earliest varieties begin to flower during the last week in May.

---

1. Published by Mr. Ridgeway, Washington, D.C., 1912.

FRAGRANCE

Fragrance is so largely a matter of personal preference that I hesitate to mention it in my list. The American Peony Society has adopted a plan of marking fragrance as follows: pleasant odour, single, double or triple X; unpleasant odour, single, double or triple X. I have found these descriptions misleading and, as the sense of smell is extremely variable, I fear others may likewise be disappointed. For example, Madame D. Treyeran is marked by the Society: "Fragrance, pleasant, XXX." In my opinion this flower has merely the suggestion of a pleasant odour. In my Main List I have simply marked those that are fragrant with an X. This runs the entire gamut from a pleasant freshness of odour up to intoxicating fragrance. The degree of sweetness had best be decided by the prospective purchaser according to his own keenness of perception of perfume values. When scent is lacking I have made no note. I have not included any positively ill-smelling varieties except Marie Jacquin, and there are some people who consider it a fragrant peony, which brings us back to where we started.

Single varieties are usually lacking in perfume and frequently have a disagreeable odour. Mr. A. H. Fewkes has made some very careful observations and drawn some interesting conclusions in this matter of fragrance in the peony. He notes that sweet odour follows closely upon the development in breeding of the stamens into petals, and that the full double (rose type) is the most fragrant. In the single and semi-double varieties the pungence of the pollen overcomes the fragrance of such few petals as there are. Mr. Fewkes also calls attention to the fact that colour has some mysterious influence upon perfume, and that the full double rose-pink varieties are the most fragrant, while the single or semi-double reds are inclined to be ill smelling, and the full double reds, in most instances, lack odour entirely.[2]

---

2. See Bulletin of Peony News, No. 2, published by American Peony Society, May, 1916.

Six Short Lists

List A
Twelve Fine White Peonies

Avalanche
Baroness Schroeder
Duchesse de Nemours
Festiva Maxima
James Kelway
La Tendresse

Madame Crousse
Marie Jacquin
Marie Lemoine
Mireille
Monsieur Dupont
Stephania

List B
Twelve Fine Pale Pink Peonies

Aurore
Eugenie Verdier
Germaine Bigot
Livingstone
Madame Lemonier
Marie Crousse

Marguerite Gerard
Milton Hill
Reine Hortense
Simonne Chevalier
Tourangelle
Venus

List C
Eight Fine Deep Pink Peonies

Alexandre Dumas
Auguste Villaume
Claire Dubois
Madame Geissler
Modele de Perfection

Monsieur Jules Elie
Souvenir de l'Exposition
  Universelle
Suzanne Dessert

List D
Twelve Fine Red Peonies

Adolphe Rousseau
Delachei
Felix Crousse
General de Boisdeffre
Grover Cleveland
Karl Rosenfield

Madame Bucquet
Madame Mechin
Monsieur Martin Cahuzac
Pierre Dessert
Raphael
Rubens

LIST E

TWELVE PEONIES OF DISTINCTION AND BEAUTY AT LOW COST

Asa Gray	Madame Calot
Couronne d'Or	Madame de Galhau
Duc de Wellington	Madame de Vatry
Grandiflora Nivea Plena	Madame de Verneville
Lamartine (Calot)	Mathilde de Roseneck
La Rosière	Solfatare

LIST F

TWELVE RARE AND EXQUISITE PEONIES

Alsace-Lorraine	Mary Woodbury Shaylor
Gismonda	Primevere
Kelway's Glorious	Sarah Bernhardt (Lemoine)
Le Cygne	Solange
Madame Jules Dessert	Thérèse
Martha Bulloch	Walter Faxon

MAIN LIST OF PEONIES

1	2	3	4	5	6	7	8	9	10
Name of variety and notes thereon	Introducer and year	Type	List	Colour effect	Size of bloom	Season	Fra-grance	Habit of growth	Special value
ADOLPHE ROUSSEAU One of the darkest peonies. Beautiful shade of garnet, very glossy petals which reflect light.	Dessert & Mechin, 1890	Semi-double	D	Garnet	Very large	Early	..	Very tall, vigorous grower, long strong stem, dark foliage, veins in leaves red. Free bloomer.	Garden
AGNES MARY KELWAY Light pink guards surround a thick cream white collar of narrow petaloids. Crown same colour as guards.	Kelway	Crown	..	Light pink	Large	Early mid-season	X	Tall, vigourous, erect. Free bloomer.	Garden and cutting
ALBERT CROUSSE Large full blooms of light salmon pink. Petals small and closely packed.	Crousse, 1893	Bomb	..	Light pink	Very large	Late	X	Tall, erect, free bloomer.	Garden and cutting
ALEXANDRE DUMAS Guards and crown bright pink. Collar of deep cream or chamois colour.	Guerin, 1862	Crown	C	Bright pink	Large and full	Mid-season	X	Medium height, free and reliable bloomer.	Cutting
ALFRED DE MUSSET Well-formed flower of pale flesh pink and salmon. One of the pinks without a hint of mauve.	Crousse, 1885	Rose	..	Flesh pink	Large	Mid-season	..	Medium height, rather spreading habit	Garden and cutting
ALICE DE JULVECOURT (Syn. Triumphans Gaudavensis) Well-built full flower. Guards and crown light pink with red streaks. Collar creamy white.	Pele, 1857	Crown	..	Pink and cream	Medium	Mid-season	X	Medium height, rather spreading habit. Fairly free bloomer.	Garden and cutting

MAIN LIST OF PEONIES (CONTINUED)

1 Name of variety and notes thereon	2 Introducer and year	3 Type	4 List	5 Colour effect	6 Size of bloom	7 Season	8 Fra- grance	9 Habit of growth	10 Special value
ALSACE-LORRAINE Pointed petals arranged like a water-lily. Flower rather flat. Colouring of cream to brownish yellow is very unusual and beautiful.	Lemoine, 1906	Semi-rose	F	Cream white deepening to yellow	Very large	Late	..	Tall, vigorous, free bloomer.	Garden and cutting
ASA GRAY Extremely full flower of pale flesh colour, with tiny dots and splashes of a deeper tint of flesh sprinkled evenly all over petals. Very striking and effective.	Crousse, 1886	Semi-rose	E	Light pink	Very large	Mid- season	X	Tall, vigorous and upright. Profuse and sure bloomer.	Garden and cutting
AUGUSTE VILLAUME Globular flower, very compact, even shade of deep pink.	Crousse, 1895	Rose	C	Deep pink	Very large	Late	..	Tall, strong grower. Buds occasionally refuse to open.	Garden
AUGUSTIN D'HOUR (Syn. Marechal MacMahon) Guard petals broad. Centre petals narrow, built up close and high, forming a large ball.	Calot, 1867	Bomb	..	Deep rich red	Very large	Late	..	Medium tall strong stiff stems, dark glossy foliage. Fairly free bloomer.	Garden
AURORE Cup-shaped flower of lovely pale pink, which fades rapidly. Sta-	Dessert, 1904	Semi-rose	B	Pale pink	Large	Late mid- season	..	Medium tall, strong stems. Good bloomer.	Cutting

Name / Description	Originator, date	Type		Colour	Size	Season		Plant	Use
Perfectly formed flower, large thick milk-white petals edged with a hair line of red, and packed solidly together. Fragrant. There is a difference of opinion among growers as to whether Avalanche and Albatre are identical. Dessert, the greatest living authority on the peony, claims that they are one and the same flower.	1886				solid			stiff stems. Free bloomer.	
AVANTE GARDE Pale rose petals veined plum colour. Bright golden stamens. One of the Wittmaniana hybrids. See Chapter 4.	Lemoine	Single	::	Pale pink	Medium	Very early	::	Vigorous, erect. Very stiff stems. Large luxuriant foliage.	Cutting
BARONESS SCHROEDER Globular flower of large white petals tinged faintly with palest pink. Petals not of great substance.	Kelway, 1889	Rose	A	White	Very large	Late	X	Tall, strong, vigorous. Free bloomer.	Garden and cutting
BEAUTE DE VILLECANTE Guards and crown pale rose. Collar pale silvery pink.	Gombault, 1856	Crown	::	Pale pink	Medium	Mid-season	X	Medium height, strong and free bloomer.	Garden and cutting
BOULE DE NEIGE Full ball of white petals tinged with sulphur colour. Guards and centre have large splashes of crimson. Stamens show throughout flower.	Calot, 1862	Semi-rose	::	White	Large	Early mid-season	X	Tall, erect, vigorous grower, free bloomer. Handsome dark foliage.	Garden and cutting
BRIDESMAID (Syns. Marie Jacquin and Water Lily) See Marie Jacquin.									

1	2	3	4	5	6	7	8	9	10
Name of variety and notes thereon	Introducer and year	Type	List	Colour effect	Size of bloom	Season	Fragrance	Habit of growth	Special value
CLAIRE DUBOIS Fine flower of deep pink tinged with mauve throughout. Large petals. Tips silvered.	Crousse, 1886	Rose	C	Deep pink	Large	Late	..	Tall, erect, strong grower.	Garden and cutting
COURONNE D'OR Very full flower, with a ring of yellow stamens around tuft of petals in the centre. Petals in tuft edged with red.	Calot, 1872	Semi-rose	E	White	Large	Late	X	Medium height, strong grower, free bloomer.	Garden and cutting
DE CANDOLLE Bright red with purplish tinge. Striking and vivid in effect.	Crousse, 1880	Rose	..	Red	Large	Mid-season	..	Medium height, strong erect grower, free bloomer.	Good for massing
DELACHEI Full and large flower. Fine shade of red.	Delache, 1856	Rose	D	Red	Large	Late	X	Medium height, strong, erect. Free bloomer.	Garden—good for massing
DR. BRETONNEAU (Syn. Lady Leonora Bramwell) Soft pink with cream white petals in centre. Sometimes splashed with crimson.	Verdier, 1854	Bomb	..	Pink	Medium	Early	X	Vigorous grower and free bloomer.	Garden and cutting
DR. BRETONNEAU Very full flower. Pale pink guards surround cream white petals tinted amber.	Guerin, 1850	Rose	..	Pink and cream	Large	Mid-season	X	Tall strong grower. Free bloomer.	Garden and cutting
DORCHESTER (Syn. Geo. W. Tryon) Light clear pink, cream and yellow in centre.	Richardson, 1870	Rose	..	Pink and cream	Medium	Mid-season to late	X	Medium tall, strong, erect. Free bloomer	Garden and cutting
DUC DE WELLINGTON Full flower. Guard petals white and broad. Centre petals nar-	Calot, 1859	Bomb	E	White	Large	Late	X	Tall, vigorous. Strong stems. Free bloomer.	Garden and cutting

Name	Originator	Type		Colour	Size	Season		Habit	Use
DUCHESSE DE NEMOURS (Syn. Mrs. Gwyn Lewis) Guard petals white, centre greenish yellow when the cup-shaped flower first opens. Develops into a large full flower which fades to white.	Calot, 1856	Crown	A	White	Medium	Early	X	Tall, strong grower and free bloomer.	Garden and cutting
DUCHESSE D'ORLEANS Guards deep bright pink. Centre pale pink and salmon.	Guerin, 1846	Bomb	::	Pink	Medium to large	Mid-season	X	Tall, strong. Free bloomer.	Garden and massing
EDULIS SUPERBA Bright mauve pink. An old garden favourite because of its fragrance and earliness.	Lemon, 1824	Crown	::	Deep pink	Large	Early	X	Strong, upright. Free bloomer.	Garden and massing
EUGENIE VERDIER Enormous flower with loose petals of flesh colour. Creamy pink shading to white in centre.	Calot, 1864	Semi-rose	B	Pale pink to white	Large	Mid-season	X	Long stems, somewhat drooping in habit, free bloomer.	Garden and cutting
FELIX CROUSSE (Syn. Victor Hugo) Clear brilliant red without violet or purple tinge. Guards and centre same colour.	Crousse, 1881	Bomb	D	Red	Medium	Mid-season	X	Medium height, strong vigorous grower, free bloomer.	Garden
FESTIVA MAXIMA Finely formed flower of large white petals. Centre petals splashed with red. Have grown Festiva Maxima in my garden with blooms 9 inches across.	Miellez, 1851	Rose	A	White	Very large	Early	X	Tall, strong, vigorous. Free bloomer. Foliage massive.	Garden and cutting
FLAG OF WAR Beautiful clear shade of dark red entirely without bluish tinge. Mass of gold stamens in centre. Keeps unusually well for a single.	Kelway	Single	::	Red	Medium	Early	::	Medium height, strong and erect. Stems reddish. Free bloomer.	Garden and cutting
FLORAL TREASURE Full ball-shaped flower of pale pink with salmon tints.	Rosenfield, 1900	Rose	::	Pink	Very large	Mid-season	X	Tall, strong, erect. Free bloomer. Pale green foliage.	Garden and cutting

1	2	3	4	5	6	7	8	9	10
Name of variety and notes thereon	Introducer and year	Type	List	Colour effect	Size of bloom	Season	Fragrance	Habit of growth	Special value
FRANCES SHAYLOR High-built bloom the colour of rich Jersey cream. Centre petals edged with deep gold. A beautiful new variety.	Shaylor, 1909	Rose	..	Cream	Medium	Late	..	Medium height, extra stiff stems. Very free bloomer.	Cutting and garden
FRANCES WILLARD Large striking flower of good substance. Fine white of the same tint as Marie Lemoine. Has faint tinge of pink on first opening.	Brand, 1907	Semi-rose	..	White	Large	Mid-season to late	X	Medium height, strong grower. Extremely free bloomer.	Garden and cutting
GENERAL DE BOISDEFFRE Very large flower of bright red. Compact, round.	Crousse, 1896	Bomb	D	Red	Large	Late	X	Strong, erect, vigorous.	Garden and cutting
GEO. W. TRYON (Syn. Dorchester—which see.)									
GERMAINE BIGOT Exquisite shade of flesh pink with centre petals splashed with red.	Dessert, 1902	Crown	B	Pale pink	Very large	Mid-season	..	Medium height, strong and erect. Free bloomer.	Garden and cutting
GIGANTEA (Syn. Lamartine-Calot—which see.)									
GISMONDA A most unusual and beautiful peony. Petals of great substance. Upper half of flower deep flesh pink. Lower half palest rose. The two colours are so clearly divided that the bloom seems composed of two flowers. Exceedingly fragrant.	Crousse, 1895	Rose	F	Pink	Very large	Late	X	Tall, strong, erect. Fine foliage. Free bloomer.	Garden and cutting

Description	Originator	Type	Grade	Color	Size	Season	Fragrant	Habit	Use
Rather small flower, extra full. Guards and crown pale rose. Collar of narrow short petals bright yellow fading to deep cream.	1866	Rose	..	yellow	medium	season	..	stems. Free bloomer.	Cutting
GRANDIFLORA Flat flower of even light rose pink. Eight or nine inches in diameter when established and well cultivated. Flowers bend over on stems.	Richardson, 1885	Rose	..	Pink	Very large	Late	X	Very tall. Stems somewhat weak.	Garden and cutting
GRANDIFLORA NIVEA PLENA Full creamy flower tinged sulphur and salmon. Touches of red in centre. An old favourite in gardens.	Lemon, 1824	Rose	E	White	Large	Early	X	Medium height. Strong grower. Free bloomer.	Cutting
GROVER CLEVELAND Large compact dark red flower.	Terry	Rose	D	Red	Large	Late	..	Medium height. Fairly strong grower. Uncertain bloomer.	Garden and cutting
HELENE LESLIE Large white guard petals. Centre sulphur yellow. Odour of a rose.	Barr	Crown	..	White and yellow	Large	Mid-season	X	Tall, free bloomer. Strong grower.	Cutting
JAMES KELWAY Beautiful broad petals, tinged with palest rose. Base of petals yellow. Golden stamens show in centre.	Kelway	Semi-rose	A	White	Very large	Mid-season	X	Medium to tall, vigorous grower.	Cutting
JESSIE SHAYLOR Very evenly formed flower. Delicate flesh changing to light cream. Exquisite fragrance. A lovely new peony, first placed on the market in 1916.	Shaylor, 1909	Rose	..	White	Large	Mid-season	X	Tall, strong, erect. Free bloomer.	Cutting and garden
KARL ROSENFIELD Rich velvety crimson, brilliant and striking. One of the very best reds.	Rosenfield, 1908	Semi-rose	D	Red	Very large	Early	..	Very tall, strong, erect grower. Free bloomer.	Garden and cutting

1	2	3	4	5	6	7	8	9	10
Name of variety and notes thereon	Introducer and year	Type	List	Colour effect	Size of bloom	Season	Fra-grance	Habit of growth	Special value
KELWAY'S GLORIOUS Enormous glistening white flower. Touch of pink on outer petals. Flower has fairy-like appearance. Petals not of great substance.	Kelway, 1909	Rose	F	White	Very large	Early mid-season	X	Medium height to tall. Strong grower, free bloomer. Fine foliage.	Cutting
LADY ALEXANDRA DUFF Loosely built bloom. Central petals touched red. Lateral flowers are semi-double, showing stamens prominently. Pale blush pink on opening, it fades rapidly to white.	Kelway, 1902	Rose	::	White	Large	Early mid-season	X	Tall, strong, free bloomer.	Garden and cutting
LADY LEONORA BRAMWELL (Syn. Dr. Bretonneau-Verdier—which see.)									
LA FÉE Unusual flower of mauve, rose and white, with extra large petals. Extremely fragrant. One of the tallest peonies grown, easily measuring 4 feet 6 inches or more.	Lemoine, 1906	Crown	::	Pink	Very large	Early	X	Extremely tall. Often between 4 and 5 feet. Free bloomer.	Garden and cutting
LA FIANCÉE Creamy white. Yellow reflection at base of petals. Centre petals touched with red. Stamens show in high crown.	Lemoine, 1898	Crown	::	White	Large	Mid-season	::	Tall, strong, vigorous grower. Not very free bloomer.	Garden and cutting
LA FRANCE Extremely large, full, rather flat flower of great substance. Petals of pale pink, guard petals	Lemoine, 1901	Rose	::	Pink	Very large	Late	X	Tall, strong, erect. Free bloomer.	Garden and cutting

Name / Description	Raiser, Date	Form		Colour	Size	Season		Habit	Use
(Syn. Gigantea) Full flower of pale silvery pink. Petals very large. Unusual and refreshing fragrance, well described as "spicy."	1860					season		Free bloomer.	Garden and cutting
LAMARTINE Compact flower of deep rose colour. Flower so large that it bends on the strong stems.	Lemoine, 1908	Rose	:	Pink	Very large	Late	X	Tall, strong, erect grower. Fairly free bloomer.	Garden and cutting
LA PERLE Globular pale pink flowers. Petals vary in depth of colour.	Crousse, 1885	Rose	:	Pink	Large	Mid-season	X	Tall, vigorous grower. Free bloomer.	Garden and cutting
LA ROSIÈRE Cup-shaped flower of creamy white, stamens showing in centre. Quite distinct in appearance.	Crousse, 1888	Semi-double	E	White	Medium	Mid-season	:	Medium height, rather spreading habit, fairly free bloomer.	Garden and cutting
LA TENDRESSE Full milk white flower. Petals of great substance. Touches of red on guard and centre petals.	Crousse, 1896	Rose	A	White	Large	Early	X	Tall, strong. Free bloomer.	Garden and cutting
LA TULIPE (Syn. Multicolore) Pinkish white petals fading rapidly to ivory white. Guard and centre petals striped with red. With cultivation reaches enormous size.	Calot, 1872	Semi-rose	:	White	Large	Mid-season	X	Tall, strong grower. Very stiff stems.	Garden and cutting
LE CYGNE Enormous ivory white flower of great beauty. Stamens occasionally visible. Petals incurved and strikingly arranged like feathers on a swan's wing. Judged by connoisseurs the finest white in the world.	Lemoine, 1907	Semi-rose	F	White	Large	Mid-season	X	Medium tall, erect, strong. Very dark green foliage. Very free bloomer.	Garden and cutting

47

1	2	3	4	5	6	7	8	9	10
Name of variety and notes thereon	Introducer and year	Type	List	Colour effect	Size of bloom	Season	Fragrance	Habit of growth	Special value
LE PRINTEMPS One of the Wittmaniana hybrids. Large flowers. A single row of thick, smooth petals pale yellow in colour. Stamens prominent. An exquisite flower. Keeps well when cut. See Chap. 4.	Lemoine	Single	..	Pale yellow	Large	Early May	..	Medium height. Vigorous growth. Foliage large, distinct and beautiful in outline and colour, which is a light green.	Cutting
LIVINGSTONE Compact flower. Soft rose pink petals with silvery edges. Keeps well when cut.	Crousse, 1879	Rose	B	Pink	Very large	Late	..	Medium height. Vigorous and erect. Free bloomer.	Garden and cutting
MADAME AUGUST DESSERT Glossy flesh colour. Centre petals lightly touched with red.	Dessert, 1899	Semi-rose	..	Creamy pink	Large	Mid-season	..	Medium height, erect. Free bloomer.	Garden and cutting
MADAME BARILLET DESCHAMPS Flat flower. Large petals of pale silvery pink. Stamens show throughout flower.	Calot, 1868	Semi-rose	..	Pink	Large	Early	X	Tall, strong grower. Has large broad leaves.	Garden and cutting
MADAME BUCQUET Clear dark red. Considered the darkest red next to M. Martin Cahuzac. A few stamens show throughout the flower.	Dessert, 1888	Semi-rose	D	Red	Medium	Mid-season	X	Medium height, strong, erect. Reddish stems. Fine foliage. Free bloomer.	Garden and cutting
MADAME CALOT Guard petals flesh pink. Centre blush and pale rose, surrounded with narrow cream white petals. On well-established plants the flowers are exquisite.	Miellez, 1856	Rose	E	White	Very large	Early	X	Tall, strong grower. Free bloomer.	Garden and cutting
MADAME CROUSSE Globular flower of clear white,	Calot, 1866	Crown	A	White	Large	Late	X	Dwarf growth. Strong, erect. Free bloomer.	Garden and cutting

Name / Description	Raiser, Year	Type		Colour	Size	Season		Habit	Use
Soft pink and salmon colouring.	1883		..		large			bloomer.	
MADAME D. TREYERAN Full flower of rosy white, freely splashed with red.	Dessert, 1889	Semi-rose	..	White	Medium to large	Early	X	Dwarf, erect. Free bloomer.	Garden and cutting
MADAME DE VATRY Guards and crown white tinged with pale pink. Collar of wide, white petals tinged with sulphur. Centre petals splashed red.	Guerin, 1853	Crown	E	White and pink	Large	Mid-season	X	Medium height. Fairly strong stems. Free bloomer.	Garden and cutting
MADAME DE VERNEVILLE Guard petals creamy white. Centre white with blush tinge when flower first opens. Centre petals sometimes edged with red.	Crousse, 1885	Bomb	E	White	Large	Early	X	Medium height. Somewhat spreading. Very free bloomer.	Garden and cutting
MADAME DUCEL Broad guard petals, centre solid compact ball. Even shade of silvery rose pink throughout.	Mechin, 1880	Bomb	..	Pink	Large	Early	X	Medium height. Strong grower, with fine dark green foliage. Free bloomer.	Garden and cutting
MADAME EMILE GALLE Flat flower. Large pale pink petals changing to white in centre. Delicate and lovely colour which fades rapidly.	Crousse, 1881	Rose	..	Pink	Large	Late	..	Tall, strong, erect. Foliage beautiful soft green. Free bloomer.	Garden and cutting
MADAME EMILE LEMOINE Large full round flower, petals closely overlapping. Glossy white tinged pale pink and covered with tiny dots of a deeper shade. The pink colouring fades rapidly and when the flower is fully open it is white.	Lemoine, 1899	Semi-rose	..	White	Very large	Mid-season	..	Medium height to tall. Strong grower and good bloomer.	Cutting
MADAME GEISSLER Massive flower of mauve pink with silvery sheen. Keeps unusually well when cut. An imposing flower. One of the largest of all peonies.	Crousse, 1880	Rose	C	Pink	Very large	Mid-season	X	Medium height. Spreading habit, as stems are not strong enough to support the enormous flowers. Free bloomer.	Cutting

1	2	3	4	5	6	7	8	9	10
Name of variety and notes thereon	Introducer and year	Type	List	Colour effect	Size of bloom	Season	Fra-grance	Habit of growth	Special value
MADAME JULES DESSERT Large flower of fine form. White petals tinged straw and flesh colour. Centre petals waved, and touched with red. Golden stamens show throughout, giving a soft glow to flower. Pointed buds. This flower should be opened in the house to secure its full beauty.	Dessert, 1909	Rose	F	White	Large	Late	..	Medium height to tall. Strong grower. Free bloomer.	Cutting
MADAME LEMOINE Large compact flower. Guards and crown white, tinged with pink. Collar milk white.	Calot, 1864	Crown	..	White	Large	Mid-season	X	Tall, strong, erect. Free bloomer.	Cutting
MADAME LEMONIER Very full flower of exquisite pale rose pink. Petals very large and glossy. The size of this peony, its great height, robust habit and fine colour make it a most striking garden subject.	Calot, 1860	Rose	B	Pink	Large	Mid-season	..	Very tall, strong and erect. Free bloomer.	Garden and cutting
MADAME MECHIN Compact flower of deep glossy garnet. One of the good reds.	Mechin, 1880	Semi-rose	D	Red	Medium	Mid-season	..	Medium height and strength. Uncertain bloomer.	Garden
MADEMOISELLE ROUSSEAU Guard petals milk white. Centre petals sulphur white with faint tinge of pink. Centre petals have	Crousse, 1888	Semi-rose	..	White	Large	Mid-season	..	Medium height. Strong and erect. Free bloomer.	Garden and cutting

Description	Raiser, date	Type		Colour	Size	Season		Habit	Use
One of the Wittmaniana hybrids. Large white flowers, tinted salmon pink, and veined at base of petals with dark violet. See Chap. 4.						May	X	strong foliage of bronze green.	Garden and cutting
MARCELLE DESSERT Creamy white with pale pink spots and some red in the centre. A fresh and delicate flower, with delightful perfume.	Dessert, 1899	Crown	..	White	Large	Mid-season	X	Medium height. Free bloomer.	Garden and cutting
MARECHAL MACMAHON (Syn. Augustin d'Hour—which see.)									
MARGUERITE GERARD Palest rose pink fading rapidly to white. Centre petals flecked with dark red. Some stamens showing.	Crousse, 1892	Semi-rose	B	Pale pink or white	Large	Late	..	Medium height. Strong erect. Free bloomer.	Garden and cutting
MARIE CROUSSE Full, perfect flower of soft salmon pink, a rare and wonderful shade. A most lovely peony to which no mere description can do justice.	Crousse, 1892	Bomb	B	Pink	Large	Mid-season	..	Tall, strong, erect grower. Free bloomer.	Garden and cutting
MARIE JACQUIN (Syns. Bridesmaid, Kelway, and Water Lily, Barr.) Cup-shaped flowers which retain this shape. The glossy white petals curve in over a centre packed with yellow stamens. On newly set plants the flowers are often single, and on well-established plants the blooms are frequently full double.	Verdier	Semi-double	A	White	Large	Mid-season	..	Medium habit. Strong, erect. Free bloomer.	Garden

MAIN LIST OF PEONIES (CONTINUED)

1	2	3	4	5	6	7	8	9	10
Name of variety and notes thereon	Introducer and year	Type	List	Colour effect	Size of bloom	Season	Fragrance	Habit of growth	Special value
MARIE LEMOINE Massive ball-shaped flower of ivory white. Some petals edged with thread of red.	Calot, 1869	Rose	A	White	Large	Late	..	Medium height. Erect and strong. Not a free bloomer.	Garden and cutting
MARTHA BULLOCH Extremely large flower. Centre deep rose pink. Outer petals shell pink. One of the fine new peonies.	Brand, 1907v	Rose	F	Deep pink	Very large	Late	X	Tall, strong and erect. Moderate bloomer.	Garden. Especially good for cutting
MARY WOODBURY SHAYLOR Guard petals clear pink. Centre petals cream, deepening to canary yellow at heart. One of the fine new peonies.	Shaylor, 1910	Rose	F	White	Medium	Mid-season	X	Dwarf. Stiff stems. Free bloomer. Broad handsome foliage.	Garden and cutting
MATHILDE DE ROSENECK Soft rose pink—centre deeper shade of rose. Very full flower.	Crousse, 1883	Rose	E	Pink	Large	Late	X	Very tall. Strong grower and free bloomer. Buds tight and slow to open.	Garden and cutting
MESSAGERE One of the Wittmaniana hybrids. Single row of white petals tinted cream. Stamens prominent. Flower cup-shaped.	Lemoine	Single	..	White	Medium large	Early May	..	Tall growth, strong dark green foliage.	Cutting
MILTON HILL Large compact flower of soft clear flesh colour. Fades rapidly in the sun. Form very beautiful. Centre petals arranged like those of a	Richardson	Rose	B	Pink	Large	Late	..	Medium to tall. Strong grower. Free bloomer.	Cutting

Variety / Description	Originator	Form		Colour	Size	Season		Habit	Use
Massive compact flower of pure white. Extremely fragrant. Impressive in appearance, and of value because of its extreme lateness.	1894							Free bloomer.	Garden and cutting
MISS SALWAY Very large, globular compact flower. Guards and crown pale tint of rose white, collar paler. Fades rapidly to white. Fragrant.	Kelway, 1905	Crown	..	White	Very large	Mid-season	X	Tall, strong grower. Free bloomer.	Garden and cutting
MODELE DE PERFECTION Very large well-formed flower. On opening flower is cup-shaped, then develops a high pointed centre. Rose pink somewhat deeper in the centre.	Crousse, 1875	Rose	C	Pink	Very large	Late	X	Medium height. Strong erect grower. Free bloomer.	Garden and cutting
MODESTE GUERIN Large compact flower. Deep bright pink, solid colour throughout.	Guerin, 1845	Bomb	..	Deep pink	Large	Mid-season	X	Medium height. Strong, erect. Free bloomer. Fine foliage.	Garden and cutting
MONSIEUR DUPONT Creamy white cup-shaped flower. Centre petals surrounded with ring of stamens. A few centre petals tipped with red.	Calot, 1872	Semi-rose	A	White	Large	Mid-season	X	Tall, erect. Strong grower. Free bloomer.	Cutting
MONSIEUR JULES ELIE Very large compact flower of deep pink with silvery sheen over entire flower. Very large petals which are a more intense pink at the base.	Crousse, 1888	Crown	C	Pink	Very large	Early mid-season	X	Medium height. Strong grower. Glossy light green foliage.	Cutting
MONSIEUR MARTIN CAHUZAC This is the darkest red peony. A deep dark garnet in colour. Petals so glossy as to appear varnished.	Dessert, 1899	Semi-rose	D	Dark red	Small to medium	Early mid-season	..	Medium height. Strong erect grower. Dark green leaves edged with red. Reddish stems. Fairly free bloomer.	Garden and cutting

MAIN LIST OF PEONIES (CONTINUED)

1	2	3	4	5	6	7	8	9	10
Name of variety and notes thereon	Introducer and year	Type	List	Colour effect	Size of bloom	Season	Fragrance	Habit of growth	Special value
MRS. GWYN LEWIS (Syn. Duchesse de Nemours—which see.)			∶						
MRS. MCKINLEY Mauve pink guard petals. Narrow centre petals yellow tinted pink.	Terry	Japanese	∶	Pink and yellow	Large	Mid-season	X	Medium height, erect, strong growth.	Garden and cutting
MULTICOLORE (Syn. La Tulipe—which see.)									
OCTAVIE DEMAY Very large full flower. Rose pink. Fades very rapidly unless cut in bud. Valuable because early.	Calot, 1867	Crown	∶	Pink	Very large	Early	X	Dwarf, erect, strong. Free bloomer.	Cutting
PHILIPPE RIVOIRE Very dark crimson flowers of good form. Extremely fragrant.	Riviere, 1911	Rose	∶	Red	Medium	Mid-season	X	Tall, stiff stems. Shy bloomer	Garden and cutting
PHILOMELE Guards and crown rose pink. Wide collar of narrow bright yellow petals. Crown is edged with red. Crown does not appear when flower first opens, and does not appear at all on weak blooms.	Calot, 1861	Japanese or crown	∶	Pink and yellow	Small to medium	Mid-season	X	Tall, strong, erect. Free bloomer.	Garden
PIERRE DESSERT Rather loosely built flower of dark garnet.	Dessert and Mechin, 1890	Semi-rose	D	Red	Large	Early	∶	Medium tall and strong. Uncertain bloomer.	Garden
PIERRE DUCHARTRE Large cup-shaped flower, closely packed with petals. Flesh pink	Crousse, 1895	Rose	∶	Pink	Large	Late	∶	Medium height. Erect strong grower.	Garden and cutting

54

Cup-shaped flower of soft pale pink.	Co., 1909				large	season	X	bloomer.	Garden and cutting
PRIMEVERE One of the few yellow peonies. Guards cream colour, with touches of red. Centre sulphur yellow.	Lemoine, 1907	Bomb	F	Yellow	Large	Mid-season	X	Tall, strong, erect grower. Free bloomer.	Garden and cutting
PRINCESS MAY (Syn. Venus—which see.)									
RAPHAEL Clear dark red. One of the few fine reds in the long list of peonies. Valuable because it blooms so early in the season.	Mechin, 1882	Semi-rose	D	Red	Medium	Early	::	Dwarf, strong, erect grower. Shy bloomer.	Garden
REINE HORTENSE Full, well-formed flower. Even shade of pale rose pink. Strikingly beautiful.	Calot, 1857	Semi-rose	B	Pink	Very large	Mid-season	X	Very tall, strong and erect. Free and reliable bloomer.	Garden and cutting
ROSA BONHEUR Large flat flower with petals overlapping. Delicate flesh pink. Guards splashed red.	Dessert	Rose	::	Pink	Very large	Mid-season	::	Tall, erect, strong grower.	Garden and cutting
ROSE D'AMOUR Large full flower—soft flesh pink. Very beautiful colour.	Calot, 1857	Bomb	::	Pale pink	Large	Mid-season	X	Tall, rather spreading. Shy bloomer	Cutting
RUBENS Clear dark red. Similar in form to Marie Jacquin.	Delache, 1854	Semi-double	D	Red	Medium	Early	X	Medium height. Fairly strong grower. Uncertain bloomer.	Garden
RUBRA SUPERBA Clear dark red without any purple tinge. Good colour. Valuable because of its lateness.	Richardson, 1871	Rose	::	Red	Large	Very late	X	Tall, erect strong grower, but not a free bloomer.	Especially good for cutting

1	2	3	4	5	6	7	8	9	10
Name of variety and notes thereon	Introducer and year	Type	List	Colour effect	Size of bloom	Season	Fra-grance	Habit of growth	Special value
RUBRA TRIUMPHANS Brilliant dark red.	Delache, 1854	Semi-double	..	Red	Large	Mid-late	..	Medium tall. Strong grower. Foliage very dark green, stems reddish. Inexpensive and excellent for mass planting.	Landscape and garden
SARAH BERNHARDT Flower of very beautiful form, with large overlapping petals. Colour a moderately deep pink.	Lemoine, 1906	Semi-rose	F	Pink	Large	Late	X	Tall, erect strong grower. Free bloomer.	Garden and cutting
SIMONNE CHEVALIER Large, globular, compact bloom. Soft salmon pink.	Dessert, 1902	Crown	B	Light pink	Large	Early	X	Very tall strong grower. Free bloomer. Beautiful foliage	Cutting
SOLANGE Wonderfully beautiful and unusual flower. Thick overlapping petals of deep cream with amber tinge. Heart of bloom has salmon shading.	Lemoine, 1907	Crown	F	Pale amber and pink	Very large	Late	..	Medium height, strong erect grower. Usually a free bloomer. Occasionally an extremely solid bud refuses to open.	Cutting
SOLFATARE Guard petals deep cream. Centre, on first opening, sulphur yellow. Fades rapidly. Well worth having in spite of its capricious habit of blooming.	Calot, 1861	Bomb	E	Yellow, fading to white	Large	Mid-season	..	Medium height. Spreading habit. Uncertain bloomer.	Cutting. Should be cut in bud or immediately upon opening
SOUVENIR DE L'EXPOSITION UNIVERSELLE Very large brilliant pink flower of fine form. Petals tipped with sil-	Calot, 1867	Rose	C	Deep pink	Very large	Late	X	Medium height. Spreading habit. Free bloomer.	Cutting

Name / Description	Raiser, year	Type		Colour	Size	Season		Habit	Use
STANLEY Dark brilliant red. Do not confuse with Stanley (Crousse).				Red	Large	...season		...erect, very free bloomer. Stems red	Garden and cutting
STEPHANIA Full cup-shaped flower, deep cream petals. Stamens show throughout, giving a golden light to flower.	Terry, 1891	Semi-double	A	Deep cream	Large	Mid-season	X	Tall, erect, strong grower. Free bloomer.	Garden and cutting
SUZANNE DESSERT Large full flower, broad glossy petals tipped with silver.	Dessert and Mechin, 1890	Semi-rose	C	Mauve pink	Very large	Mid-season	..	Tall, strong, erect grower. Good bloomer.	Garden
THE BRIDE Guard petals have pink tinge. Centre milk white.	Terry	Bomb	..	White	Medium	Mid-season	..	Medium height, strong grower, rather spreading habit. Very free bloomer.	Especially good for landscape
THÉRÈSE Full double flower of glossy flesh colour, somewhat paler in the centre. One of the very finest peonies.	Dessert, 1904	Rose	F	Pink	Very large	Mid-season	..	Tall, strong, erect. Free bloomer.	Garden and cutting
TOURANGELLE Delicate rose pink.	Dessert, 1910	Rose	B	Pink	Large	Late	..	Medium height. Strong grower. Free bloomer.	Cutting
TRIUMPHANS GAUDAVENSIS (Syn. Alice de Julvecourt—which see.)									
TRIOMPHE DE L'EXPOSITION DE LILLE Full flower of fine form. Soft flesh pink with tiny splashes of deep rose. One of the best inexpensive pinks.	Calot, 1865	Semi-rose	..	Pale pink	Very large	Mid-season	..	Medium height. Strong grower and free bloomer.	Cutting

MAIN LIST OF PEONIES (CONTINUED)

1	2	3	4	5	6	7	8	9	10
Name of variety and notes thereon	Introducer and year	Type	List	Colour effect	Size of bloom	Season	Fra-grance	Habit of growth	Special value
UMBELLATA ROSEA (Formerly known as Sarah Bernhardt.) Large guard petals pale rose pink. Centre straw white. Roots increase rapidly and plant blooms very young.	Dessert	Rose	..	White	Medium	Early	X	Medium height. Strong grower. Very free bloomer.	Massing, garden and cutting
VENUS (Syn. Princess May.) Collar palest pink. Centre warm flesh pink.	Kelway	Crown	B	Pale pink	Large	Mid-season	X	Tall, strong, free bloomer.	Garden and cutting
VICTOR HUGO (Syn. Felix Crousse—which see.)									
WATER LILY (Syns. Marie Jacquin and Bridesmaid.) See Marie Jacquin.									
WALTER FAXON Clear bright pure pink. Outer edge of flower somewhat paler. Very double, with a few stamens showing in centre.	Richardson	Semi-rose	F	Pink	Small to medium	Mid-season	..	Medium height. Strong free bloomer.	Cutting

Extending the Period of Bloom

T HE peony is sometimes criticised on the ground that its period of bloom is not sufficiently long. The peony does not have the characteristic of other perennials such as the larkspur, which, after being cut down, blossoms again the same season; nor does it bloom as continuously as the hybrid tea rose does under favourable conditions. But the dazzling gorgeousness of the flower is more than compensation for its comparatively short life.

While it is true that the flowers of an individual variety of peony will last only a number of days, it is also true that by making a judicious choice of different species and varieties it is easily possible to have the joy of peonies in one's garden for a period of six or seven weeks. Moreover, as the peony has in recent years become the subject of so much horticultural and commercial interest, it is undoubtedly only a matter of time before the scientific plant breeders, by the employment of methods of selection successfully used with other plants, will increase the sum of our happiness by lengthening the period of bloom still further.

In addition to flowering at the desired time all of the varieties suggested in this chapter for the purpose of extending the season have distinct and attractive qualities of their own.

The following list gives the approximate order of bloom of the different kinds of peonies desirable for the garden. The order, of course, will vary somewhat on account of different conditions of soil, exposure and weather.

(1) **P. tenuifolia**—with fern-like foliage.

(2) **P. Wittmaniana and Wittmaniana hybrids**—little known but very beautiful.

(3) **P. officinalis** (rubra and other varieties)—the peony of our grandmothers' gardens.

(4) **P. suffruticosa or P. moutan**—the tree peony.

(5) **P. lutea**—a pure yellow species.

(6) P. albiflora or sinensis—Chinese peonies.

Early varieties.

Midseason varieties.

Late varieties.

(1) First to bloom in the old-fashioned gardens was **P. tenuifolia**, known in England as the Adonis peony. With its fragrant flowers of bright blood-red, and its deeply cut fern-like leaves, resembling somewhat those of giant fennel, it is thoroughly in harmony with the other delicate traceries of early Spring. This graceful little plant which attains only sixteen or eighteen inches in height, still has a strong appeal, but is not planted in the modern garden as frequently as it deserves to be. A few weeks after blooming P. tenuifolia dies down to the ground and disappears until the following Spring, differing in this respect from the other species, whose foliage remains and helps to furnish the garden all Summer. There are both single and double flowered varieties: it is difficult to decide which is the more attractive.

This peony is a native of the Ukraine, Russia, a region that lies north of the Black Sea. It grows in profusion there and on the hilly grounds and steep banks of the Terek District in the Caucasus. The first mention of it was in a European catalogue published in 1757. It is thought to have been introduced into England by William Malcolm in 1765.

(2) The season of P. tenuifolia is closely followed by that of the **Wittmaniana hybrids** which bloom early in May, nearly a month ahead of the Chinese varieties. The original Wittmaniana species was probably named after Wittman, a botanist who travelled in the Caucasus. The details of its introduction are shrouded in mystery, a fact which is the more remarkable because of the novel colour of the flower—yellow. It is first mentioned in the Journal of Botany (London), for 1842, where a letter is quoted which shows that, together with other rare plants, it had been received in a garden in the Crimea, from Count Worontzoff in Adsharia, not far from Erzerum. Subsequently this species was lost for a number of years, but was rediscovered about 1880 in an obscure Irish garden. The suggestion has been made that the American Peony Society commission some horticultural Arsene Lupin to unravel the mysteries of Wittmaniana's appearance, disappearance and re-appearance.

The flower is single with large firm petals of a colour well described as "light primrose with a dash of lemon." The seeds are a bright coral red. This type species is not grown here very successfully; for some inexpli-

cable reason it often dies out.

The Wittmaniana hybrids, however, are very hardy. M. Lemoine, the French hybridist, by making crosses of various Chinese varieties on P. Wittmaniana has produced these valuable extra early-flowering sorts. They have large fragrant single flowers of great beauty, in delicate tints of white, yellow, rose and salmon, and have thick leaves of vigorous and luxuriant growth. Avante Garde, palest rose; Le Printemps, yellowish cream; Mai Fleuri, salmon white, and Messagere, sulphur white, are all most attractive.

P. Wittmaniana has also been crossed with P. Russi by Lemoine, thereby producing Russi major which, while very early-flowering, has a mauve colouring not always acceptable.

A seedling of P. Wittmaniana put out by Barr, in England, bears a single flower of soft rose and yellow tints (P. Wittmaniana rosea).

(3) The bloom of the Wittmaniana hybrids is succeeded by that of **P. officinalis**, so named because in the early days its roots were used for medicinal purposes. The variety rubra plena (double red) is the peony so common in the old-time gardens: in fact, up to about 1850 this was the only peony grown to any great extent in this country. Its large size and persistent growth, the vivid red colour of its blooms and its noticeably unpleasant odour all serve to impress its personality on the observer. For sentimental reasons and because it is one of the parents of some of the wonderfully beautiful peonies of to-day, this peony is entitled to a place in every garden.

Besides this old red "piney" there are several other fine kinds of the officinalis species that are deserving of selection. Four particularly striking varieties are easily obtainable and share with the rubra plena the merit of blooming in May. They are:

P. OFFICINALIS ALBA PLENA, which has double white flowers. The buds are pink when they appear, but fade to white as the flower opens.

P. OFFICINALIS ROSEA PLENA, which has full flowers of bright rose.

P. OFFICINALIS LOBATA.[*] This peony has single flowers of an unusual colour—a glorious orange scarlet.

P. OFFICINALIS LA NEGRESSE, which has full, double, rich, dark maroon blooms.

(4) Next in point of flowering come the tree peonies. These have as an-

---

[*] At the present time an animated controversy is going on in England as to the proper classification of lobata. There is no controversy as to the beauty of the flower.

cestors a primitive Chinese species, **P. suffruticosa or P. moutan**, and are distinguished from the herbaceous peony in having a shrub-like habit and a permanent woody growth that does not die down to the ground in the Autumn. This type has been cherished and cultivated in China and Japan for hundreds of years, and has, since 1787, received much attention in Europe—particularly in England. In many places in England, however, it is grown with but indifferent success, which is due possibly to the climate or to local conditions. It does better in eastern America, where the climate—especially of the Atlantic Coast slope of the United States—is similar to that of interior China, its original habitat. The tree peony usually reaches a height of three or four feet. There is an instance of one in England twelve feet high and thirty-six feet in circumference which never failed for twenty-five years to produce annually several hundred blooms. The flowers of P. moutan are remarkable for their beauty of form, texture and colour combined; they are also very large—often measuring from seven to ten inches across—and have a satisfactory way of lasting long on the plants. One is surprised that this species is not more appreciated and frequently planted. The history of the tree peony and some of the points to be remembered in its culture are set out in Chapters 8 and 9. Among the many fine varieties grown to-day there are at least four so exquisite that they should be in every peony lover's garden:

CAROLINE D'ITALIE, which has finely formed flowers of silvery flesh colour, with a reflex of salmon.

MME. STUART-LOW, which has cup-shaped flowers of bright salmon red with broad silvery border and golden stamens. The flowers are of exceptional brilliance and the plant blooms luxuriantly.

BLANCHE DE CHATEAU FUTU, which has flowers of pure white with carmine spots. This is also a free bloomer.

REINE ELIZABETH is considered the finest of all the tree peonies. The flowers are massive—salmon pink with brilliant copper tints. The plant is a vigorous grower and free bloomer.

(5) After P. moutan comes the bloom of **P. lutea**. This species, usually classed among the tree peonies on account of its woody stems, has thick, deeply lobed dark-green leaves and cup-shaped single flowers, measuring about three and one-half inches across, with waxy fleshy petals of a wonderful golden yellow, strong and pure. In some of the blooms the lower half of the filaments is red, giving the effect of a red ring in the centre of the flower. Curiously the leaves are of the same outline and habit of

growth as those of the tree peony, while the buds are of the same shape as those of the herbaceous peony. In addition to its beauty this little peony is gifted with fragrance, somewhat like that of a lily.

Thirty years ago Abbé Delavay—a missionary—discovered P. lutea in the Yunnan Mountains in southern China, and sent twenty-six seeds marked "Seed of an Alpine plant" to the Jardin des Plantes in Paris. Only three of the twenty-six seeds lived, but from them are descended all the P. lutea now in cultivation. From France this peony was introduced into England and thence to this country.

Two recent hybrids of P. lutea and P. moutan offer much of interest and beauty, though not as early flowering as either parent. P. L'Esperance, introduced in 1909 by Lemoine, is similar to P. moutan in foliage and habit, and has single flowers eight inches across with eight or ten broad-fringed petals, in colour soft yellow tinged with buff and splashed at the base with red. P. La Lorraine, sent out in 1912, also by Lemoine, has a very full globular bloom, about six inches across, regular in outline and of a buff tone passing to golden yellow. It gained high honours in France and was awarded the First Class Certificate—a recognition of great merit—by the English Royal Horticultural Society in 1912. It was one of the most startling novelties introduced into England in that year. This variety is not offered as yet in this country.

(6) The last to bloom and most glorious of all the peonies is **P. albiflora**. It is this peony to which reference is usually made to-day under the generic term "peony." Nearly all of the five hundred or more named double varieties of albiflora have been obtained by crossing P. albiflora (mostly single) with P. officinalis, peregrina and other species. This crossing which produced a wide range of colour and form has been the means of lengthening the blooming season for the improved species, the result of the union. Many of the best varieties of P. albiflora have been given in Chapter 3. In order to complete the plan of having peonies in flower in the garden for the longest possible time, a few of the earliest, midseason and latest varieties are here named again.

	Umbellata Rosea	white
	Festiva Maxima	white
Early ········	Madame Ducel	pink
	Mons. Jules Elie	pink
	Adolphe Rousseau	red

	Avalanche	white
	Marie Jacquin	white
Midseason ·····⎨	Madame Lemonier	pink
	Gloire de Chas. Gombault	pink and yellow
	Mons. Martin Cahuzac	red

	Marie Lemoine	white
	Baroness Schroeder	white
Late ··········⎨	Pierre Duchartre	pink
	Livingstone	pink
	Rubra Superba	red

Purchasing

U NLESS the admirer of peonies, who longs impatiently for exquisite flowers of his own, has the good fortune to be tutored by a disinterested authority, he is on the road to enrollment in the expensive school of experience—expensive to a varying degree in money, and expensive to a certain degree in time and results. Many varieties of the peonies take two to four or even in some cases five years to become so well established as to give the most typical blooms. The owner inevitably feels resentment on ultimately finding, after an extended period of care and anticipation, that the flower is of inferior quality, that it is different from what was ordered, or that possibly the plant is a shy bloomer or does not bloom at all. For months and years to slip by without bringing the development one has a right to expect is both disappointing and disheartening. As I look back to my early unguided efforts to have "lots of lovely peonies," the memory of time-consuming mistakes I made, which might have been avoided had I but had advice, encourages me to try to help others.

Successful purchasing of peonies, as of most things, resolves itself into three factors—knowing quality and prices, knowing where to get the best and knowing what one wants. In other words, the buyer of peonies who desires the satisfaction of feeling that he has used good judgment, must study (1) the difference between good and bad stock; (2) the individuals and firms in the peony business and what they offer, and (3) his own taste and requirements.

CATALOGUES

While it is often enthralling and always enlightening to secure catalogues from a number of growers and dealers and to compare the lists, both of varieties and prices, it must be remembered that the beauty of the printed matter does not always necessarily correspond with the quality of the

plants offered. Advertising is a branch of any business which is artistically or carelessly done, as its importance is or is not recognised by the advertiser. But neither the beauty nor the simplicity of the printed matter affects the varying margin between euphemism and accuracy. The general reputation for integrity of the grower or dealer putting out the catalogue is an all-important matter about which inquiry should be made.

Peony growers' booklets contain much valuable information, but they are sometimes misleading. The fascination of the printed word seems never to be so strong as in flower catalogues. The ingenuousness with which one peruses and accepts all of these that come to hand each year is undeniable proof of the vernal and eternal characteristic of hope. While catalogue reading is practically unexcelled as a form of indoor agricultural and horticultural diversion, I fear that it is somewhat dangerous to the happiness if not to the life or liberty of the novice. The extravagant use of "the best," "superb," "splendid," "magnificent," "indispensable" and other ecstatic adjectives at times thrills even a hardened buyer, but to the beginner, sensitive to suggestion, it is often positively hypnotic. I would not for a moment intimate that this is wilful misrepresentation: it does not seem, however, always to be the whole truth. A peony may be veraciously described as so appealingly beautiful that one's hand at once reaches for the order form. But before indulging the impulse and filling in the blanks, important questions should be asked and satisfactorily answered:

1. Is the coveted peony a free bloomer?
2. Are the stems strong?
3. Is its odour agreeable?
4. Is it better for cutting or for landscape?
5. Is it the proper height for the place where it is to be planted?

And after all these points are disposed of, others arise:

6. Will the stock described in the catalogue be as represented?
7. Will the roots be strong and healthy?
8. Will they be true to name?
9. What is the grower's or dealer's reputation as to reliability?

First Hand Information and Disinterested Advice

The ideal way to choose peonies is to visit several nurseries and make selections of plants when in bloom. Of the hundreds of varieties of peonies, the average general nursery carries in stock only a comparatively

small number. The growers of peonies exclusively, or of peonies in connection with a few other perennials, usually put out long lists of the finest kinds. In order to make comparisons of the habit of growth and the quality of stock, as well as to enlarge one's acquaintance with the flowers of the different varieties, it will be of advantage for one to visit a number of nurseries, whether the lists of peonies offered for sale are large or small.

A convincing reason for seeing the flowers in bloom before ordering is the fact that probably no words in the English language convey so many shades of meaning as those expressing shades of colour. When one reads in a catalogue that a certain flower is "Tyrian rose" or "Bengal rose" or "Solferino red," unless one possesses a colour chart, or is familiar with the terminology of the peony trade, or has perhaps the good fortune to have lived in Tyre, Bengal or Solferino, as the case may be, the description will probably be unintelligible. How many beginners go to the dictionary to find that "amaranth" is "a name given to mixtures of colouring matters of which the chief constituent is magenta"? Most of us, I fear, learn the definition through experience when the flower appears. One may, of course, like magenta: but if a bluish pink, or purplish red bring tears to the eyes of others as they do to mine, it is no laughing matter to own an amaranth peony.

Visits to peony exhibitions will also prove invaluable in giving the opportunity to compare colours and to determine those one likes best. Furthermore, at exhibitions one can readily and delightfully become acquainted with names of varieties and types of form.

In addition to seeing the nurseries of commercial growers and studying exhibitions, still another important source of aid lies in viewing private collections. The gardening spirit usually prompts the owners to extend assistance to other flower lovers, so that disinterested information is easily available. Even in a small garden containing a few cherished peonies, much help may be obtained. I give here a list of questions to ask of one's indulgent friends, the answers to which it will be of benefit to have and consider before buying.

1. Where and when were the roots purchased?
2. How old were they when they were bought?
3. How large were they, and did they have fat eyes?
4. Did they bloom the first year after planting?
5. If not, how many years passed before they bloomed?
6. Have they been transplanted?
7. Have they been divided?
8. Was the stock clean and healthy?

One should always note under what conditions of soil and location the peonies are planted, and in drawing conclusions one should be fair to both grower and owner.

In the Autumn, in the digging and shipping season, visits to nurseries are also instructive. One then finds out in a general way what each grower gives in return for the prices asked in his catalogue. The size and quality of roots sent out by growers vary greatly: the blooms from the roots will show a corresponding difference. Some growers list and advertise one-, two- and three-year roots. Others quote a single price and say nothing about the age or size of the roots. In the latter case one buys in ignorance and on faith: in addition, one's mind is so occupied with pictures of the glorious flower described that little thought is given the roots except as to the number required.

PRICES

In buying peonies, low prices alone should not influence the purchaser. A root of some standard variety such as Festiva maxima may be bought from some growers as low as thirty-five cents, whereas the same variety, listed as being the same age, bought from others will cost as much as sixty cents. The plants listed may both be true to name, but there are probably differences in the quality of the root which determine the price. X's root at sixty cents will begin to bloom possibly the first season, and surely the second season after planting, whereas Y's cheaper root may and probably will not be vigorous enough to bloom until the third or fourth year. And there is no certainty that it will be a fine strong flower when it does appear at last.

Three experiences recounted from notes in my garden book may be of interest from several angles.

1. Some years ago I bought from a general nurseryman and seedsman a dozen peony roots of standard varieties. As his roses and seeds had been most satisfactory, I ordered peonies from his catalogue without further thought. Two years after planting only one flower bloomed on each of two of the plants. At the end of three years these same two plants bore several flowers apiece. At the end of four years the remaining ten roots, which had not produced a solitary bloom in all this time, were pulled up, examined and destroyed. The roots were not diseased but were small and weak: in fact during the four years that they had been in my garden they had not

noticeably increased in size. Evidently the stock had been divided too often and into too small pieces, and the roots had not been able to recover their strength.

2. On another purchase of fourteen roots, which was made from a grower of peonies, I had a most disappointing experience. As this grower strongly advocated mulching with manure, I conscientiously proceeded to mulch as directed. This caused two of the roots to rot away during the first winter. At the end of one year only one flower appeared on the remaining twelve plants. At the end of two years, four plants, supposedly of one variety, bloomed well, but one of the four was not true to name. The other plants had one flower apiece, but have refused to bloom even thus luxuriantly since then. At the end of three years three more plants decided to blossom in a half-hearted way, and two others did creditably. In other words, after four years' waiting only five plants out of fourteen proved to be satisfactory.

3. The third experience makes more cheerful reading. From another grower of peonies, I secured a shipment of exceptionally fine roots. The first year after planting seventy-five per cent of these bloomed: some of the plants bore six or eight flowers. The second year all except one bloomed freely and had sturdy flowers and strong lustrous foliage. The prices for these roots were higher than those of certain other growers and nurserymen, but the results warranted the added expense. I have just come in from the garden this warm May morning after having counted with a miser's thrills of joy the many large, vigorous buds on plants furnished only last year by the same man. May he live long and prosper!

The newest and scarcest peonies command a fancy price. The wise beginner will leave the buying of these varieties until he has had either ample experience or specific expert advice. Some of them are wonderfully beautiful and desirable, and others are expensive because there are only a small number on the market, not necessarily because they are greatly superior to the well-known kinds which should be in every peony garden.

Quality is more important than quantity. It is far cheaper in the end to purchase roots of finest quality and after several years propagate them than to buy cheap roots which may be poor stock and possibly not true to name. In the first instance one has roots of ever-increasing value: in the second, after a few years of disappointment the roots will probably be thrown away, entailing a loss of time which, in peony growing, is of even more importance than money.

The ever-widening interest in the peony, and a consequently large demand for it, together with the fact that the peony increases slowly, will
probably cause the inevitable law of supply and demand to keep up the
prices of the standard varieties.

POINTS TO BE DECIDED

The decision as to where to buy may be arrived at in one of several ways.
It may be the result of observation during visits to various nurseries and
gardens, or it may be made on the advice of experienced friends, or, in the
event that observation and advice are not available, a conclusion may be
reached by doing a little experimental buying. Roots can be obtained from
each of several nurseries, and comparisons of their quality carefully made.
In Chapter 7 on Propagation . . . will be found . . . descriptions of both
healthy and sick roots, which will be of assistance in forming a judgment
on the quality and condition of stock.

Having decided where the roots are to be bought, the next step in purchasing is to determine for what use the peonies are wanted. If they are to
be planted for landscape effects the best for the purpose are the varieties
in white, strong pink and red, which colours have the advantage of fading
less in the sun. If the peonies are for the garden, varieties in any colours
may be chosen. If the flowers are to be used largely for cutting, those that
are best suited for that purpose should be selected. For planting in mixed
borders the colours of the other perennials in bloom at the same time
should be remembered. Edulis superba—pink—and scarlet Oriental poppies make a clash which can be heard for miles! All these considerations
enable one to make a choice not to be regretted or reversed, a procedure
which is usually disturbing to one's mind and purse as well as to the peonies themselves.

The number of peonies required should receive careful attention from
the novice. For one's first purchase, the smallest number with which one
can possibly manage to exist is best. Make haste slowly in collecting: it is
likely to be less expensive and it is a good deal more amusing. Two or three
years' experience will bless one with an amazing amount of wisdom, and
there will probably be a warm feeling of self-gratulation later at the restraint exercised.

As orders are filed and filled in the sequence in which they are received
at the nursery, the earlier the order is completed and sent the better. When
the order is forwarded it is well to ask whether the varieties specified can

be furnished in the quantities and ages desired. If some varieties cannot be supplied, the plan of planting may be rearranged or the order for them placed elsewhere. State in the order the date on which shipment is to go forward, and request a notice of the shipment before it is dispatched, so that arrangements can be made for being at home at the time of planting: even the most trusted gardeners sometimes make mistakes. If one cares at all for peonies their arrival, unpacking and planting will be both a rite and a festival.

CHAPTER SIX

Planting, Cultivating and Fertilizing

AMONG able gardeners the consensus of opinion is that peonies are best planted in the fall. September and October are the months generally agreed upon as the most propitious. Mid-September is the opening of the planting season in my garden. Before that time the buds on the roots are not likely to be fully formed.

Planting can be continued as long as the ground is fit to be worked, but peonies set out late in the autumn do not have the opportunity to become settled and to put forth new roots before the freezing weather overtakes them. If they are loose in the ground, they may be heaved out by the frost. Both heaving and immature root-buds affect the quality and quantity of bloom the following year.

Spring planting has been well tested out by cultivators of wide experience, and almost unanimously condemned because of the unavoidable disturbance of the early-waking roots. Occasionally a voice is raised in its favor, and some scattering catalogues advertise peonies for sale for either fall or spring planting.

I suppose that the occasional voice has some special or personal reason for its endorsement. And I presume that the firms approving of this technique also have special reasons. But the reasons, whatever they are, do not include the well-being of the peony. Certainly there is no law against spring planting. But to my mind and in the opinion of many other devotees, it is a mistake to plant peonies in the spring.

The ground where peonies are to be planted should, if it is a possible thing, be made ready several months in advance. Particularly is this necessary if unusually deep preparation of the soil is made; for the divisions or newly set plants will sink with the settling soil, and the same effect as that of too deep planting will be the result.

In ground that is fully settled and really ready, then, the roots should be placed so that the topmost eyes will be between two and three inches be-

low the level of the finished bed. This is the rule for a clay loam. In soils that are light they may be planted as deep as three or three and a half inches.

Planting that is too shallow has several disadvantages. The roots are quickly heaved out of the ground by frost. The earth is more easily washed from them by heavy rains, and thus exposed, they rot rapidly. Cultivation of the plant is more likely to injure the crowns if they are shallowly placed. Again, the crown of the peony naturally pushes upward as the plant grows older, so that in time an old root is often flush with the surface and has to be covered. If the root is originally planted too high, this condition is hastened.

On the other hand, planting that is too deep is one of the causes of shy-blooming in the peony, and for that reason should be shunned. Careful attention to the placing of the roots at the proper depth means that some thought should be given in each case to the quality of the soil.

Divisions that are very small should not be planted as deeply as standard divisions or one-year roots. A depth of two inches is ample. Indeed, such tiny pieces should receive extra care, for not only have they—like the others—suffered the shock of division, but being small, they have less strength and food in reserve upon which to call until they are established. If these little divisions are of rare and expensive varieties, as they are most likely to be, they may well be placed for the first year or two of their life in a cold-frame, or in some carefully shielded and well-drained spot. As the size of the new roots sent out by the dealers becomes smaller and smaller, so must the skill of the amateur who receives them become greater and greater, if he is to save his precious purchases.

Another important matter is the avoidance of sites where peonies have been previously planted. In such places the soil is usually exhausted. This is bound to be the case if the first tenant has been there for several years. Unless the old soil is removed and fresh rich earth put in, the new plant, even if it manages to survive, frequently fails to succeed. I mentioned this point in *The Book of the Peony* several years ago, and I have always stressed it in talks I have given. It is a pleasure to note that many of the professional growers are, in their catalogues, laying special emphasis upon the fact. Here is a little detail that may stand between failure and success.

If a number of peony roots are to be planted, they should not be closer to one another than two and a half or three feet. If ground can be spared, or if only a few specimens are to go into the garden, a greater distance may be left to advantage. Four or even five feet between roots which are to remain permanently in position is not too much to allow for growth and spreading.

The first winter after setting out the roots or divisions of ordinary size, they should be mulched (covered) to prevent their heaving out of the ground through alternate freezing and thawing. After the first season, winter protection of the peony is unnecessary except in the case of tiny divisions or young seedlings. It is well to guard these with a winter covering for two or even three years.

Salt hay, straw, cornstalks, and leaves (not peony foliage) are all good materials with which to mulch. Whichever one is used should be put on after the first hard freezing of the ground.

Manure is a deadly thing to apply as a mulch for peonies. It is still advised and still employed by some gardeners for this purpose, but I think that their number is decreasing as their experience widens. It is entirely possible to use manure freely and with apparent safety for several years. And then, some fine day, it is entirely probable that the insouciant gardener may find his peonies the prey of wilt and rot and blight! These afflictions will then have to be fought for a longer or shorter period of time until all the festive little fungus-spores, so hospitably fostered by the manure, have been conquered. Solid manure never touches my peonies. They are protected and fed by other materials.

While manure is a favorite resting- and breeding-place for fungus growths, it is not the only one. The dead leaves and stems of the peony itself, if left to mould and rot upon the ground each winter, are a fertile source of trouble. For this reason, each fall as the peony foliage ripens in my garden it is cut off and relentlessly burned. That is a big task, too, for the stalks are not dry enough to make good fuel. None the less, burn they must; and rubbish, old pieces of wood, anything that will burn freely, is mixed with them. With a dash of kerosene added, the auto-da-fé begins.

Early in the spring the peonies which were planted and mulched the previous fall should be examined. The covering should be removed in good time. Even the innocuous salt-hay or cornstalks can cause trouble if left on the beds too long under the warm rays of the spring sun. Therefore, the moment that the peonies show their "dear rosy snouts," as my friend, Miss Jekyll, calls them, the mulch must be promptly and carefully removed.

As soon as the ground is dry enough to handle, the peony beds should be thoroughly cultivated. Constant and conscientious cultivation all season long brings many rewards. In this way moisture is conserved in the soil, weeds cannot steal food from the flowers, any added fertilizer is thoroughly incorporated with the earth, ant nests are broken up and rose bugs

have no chance at all to bring up their children!

An urgent reason for the early cultivation of peonies is the occasional presence of the May beetle (Melolontha vulgaris) in the ground. These large predacious beetles hibernate in the soil, and become active with the first vernal impulses. Hungry after the winter's fast, they are capable of doing great damage to peony roots as well as to other plants. When cultivation has been unduly delayed I have known them to gnaw around and completely destroy large pieces of peony crown.

The use of fertilizers to secure more and larger blossoms is the subject of constant testing for all flowers. But just now the fertilization of peonies seems to be in a perfect fever of experiment.

Three necessary elements for the growth of all plants are nitrogen which feeds the leaves, phosphorus which feeds the stems, and potash, which is the chief source of food for the flowers and fruit.

The simplest plan for providing these in the garden is by spading in green crops or manure for nitrogen, bone meal for phosphorus, and wood ashes for potash. These applications are nature's own way of fertilizing, slightly accelerated. For the spaded green-crops are but another form of the rotted leaves of trees or grass, the bone meal but a quick return to earth of the animal life upon it, and the wood ashes but a concentrated application of the alkali salts contained within the earth itself.

Manure, which is richest in nitrogen, is of special value because it stimulates the beneficent bacteria in the soil. And while solid manure is generally unsafe for immediate use with peonies, because it is so genial a host to undesirable spores, the gardener gets around that difficulty by using manure in liquid form.

I have used, and occasionally still do use, commercial fertilizers—phosphoric acid, muriate of potash, nitrate of soda, sulphate of iron, and other chemicals—in connection with the culture of the peony; but I am convinced that such fertilization is easily overdone and that concentrated chemicals, as well as manure, should be employed with the greatest restraint. Although growers and dealers in their catalogues and planting instructions seldom mention it, the fact remains—as I have already pointed out—that the soil can readily be made too rich for the peony.

Green crops, bone meal, and wood ashes are slower than most commercial fertilizers in giving results, but they are much safer and therefore more desirable in the long run. Even these "natural" fertilizers must be used with care. Either bone meal or wood ashes will burn the roots if allowed to come into contact with them. Wood ashes are particularly valuable to

use on peonies, because the caustic effect of both the potash and the lime contained therein tends to keep the soil sweet and ward off fungous growths; but they should be raked or stirred into the soil only after the root is protected by a layer of earth.

Every once in a while I read some letter or article in which the writer protests against the disbudding of peonies.

Disbudding is the technical word for removing the lateral or side buds from a peony stalk. The result of taking off these buds is an increased size of the flower coming from the terminal bud which has been allowed to remain. Certain varieties are undeniably more decorative if left to produce sprays of small flowers instead of one big blossom on each stem. Peonies which show many stamens, La Rosière for example, are specially charming grown in this way. So are the single varieties. As a general practice, however, most peony enthusiasts prefer to secure large blooms. There is no doubt that size is an impressive feature in the general appearance of a peony. Therefore the side or lateral buds may be removed while they are still very small, in order that their strength may be diverted into the end or terminal bud. If show flowers are wanted, still greater strength and size may be obtained for them by cutting or pinching off some of the weaker shoots of the plant when they are a few inches above ground in the spring.

It is probable that there are seldom two or three peony-lovers gathered together without discussion of rose bugs—their ubiquitousness, their sins, and their possible eradication. Several prepared remedies are offered for sale, but I have yet to hear enthusiastic approval of any of them except by the salesmen.

A fellow gardener in Connecticut has solved the rose-bug problem to her own satisfaction. She finds that one ounce of powdered sulphate of iron to each square yard of surface, well worked into the ground once a month, after either a good rain or a good wetting with the hose, will at once decrease the number of rose bugs. If this treatment is continued for three successive seasons, she finds that no more rose bugs will appear.

I am inclined to think that the value of this remedy lies in the regular and thorough stirring of the soil. The young of the rose-chafer, when in the pupal stage, lie near the surface of the ground. At that period of their development the slightest disturbance kills them. Be that as it may, the treatment recommended has two certain advantages in addition to the frequent cultivation: one is that there is no nasty spray to touch the flowers, and the other is that sulphate of iron is a stimulant to the roots of the peonies, and an agent of no mean power in increasing the depth of color in the flowers.

Ants are another annoyance in the garden, and although the damage they do is so indirect that it is not always laid to their account, it is none the less real, and it is often serious. Spores of fungoid growths are carried by ants from one plant to another. This fact has been made a subject of careful experiment and undeniable proof. Large numbers of ants, seeking the honey-like substance on peony buds, are able to do untold mischief. And while they disappear to a large extent after the buds have expanded and the "honey" is gone, yet if disease is present in the near neighborhood, it was probably well spread by them before they left.

The orchard orioles destroy many ants. The old apple-trees near our house are favorite nesting-places each year for these lovely birds. Frequently I see an oriole swaying on a big peony-stalk while he lunches heartily upon ants. But the birds cannot kill all of these countless insects. We must help, too.

Several years ago Dr. Huey, the famous rosarian, told me to pour boiling water into the ants' nests whenever I found them. We do this in my garden every year. It is not a permanent cure, but it very noticeably depletes the hordes of mischief makers. Occasionally I meet one of the gardeners hurrying triumphantly along a path with a steaming teakettle in his hands. Then a detour to the back of the house brings to view an angry cook standing in the doorway and muttering maledictions! This rape of the teakettle almost precipitates internecine strife at times. For the cook thinks of the garden only as a pleasant place wherein the mistress of the house indulges an unaccountable taste for hard work, while the gardener regards the house as a mere appendage of the garden—a place of refuge during storms, and a temporary shelter each night until the real business of life—which is to garden—may be resumed again in the morning.

One of them is entirely right—but I shall not say here which it is. It might not be politic; for, after all, I need both the garden and the house for my happiness and my comfort.

Propagation

HERBACEOUS peonies are usually propagated in two ways: 1, by the division of roots, which method increases the number of plants of established varieties, and 2, by growing from seeds, which method, as the offspring never come true to either parent, produces new varieties.

DIVISION

Professional growers select stock one, two or three years old for dividing. Two-year-old stock is best. The use of young roots for division not only saves time in increasing stock, but also produces plants which flower more freely. Roots older than two years may also be successfully divided and grown: it is indeed such roots which ordinarily are divided in private gardens. As the amateur grower desires to have blooms he leaves his peonies undisturbed to flower. However, if they are left too many years before they are divided, the new stock thus secured may be disappointing. Divisions from old clumps sometimes fail to flower freely.

Young plants have straight and smooth roots and may be cut up easily and evenly; the older the plant the more difficult is the process of division. The peony root grows so large and strong that after a few years it often becomes a mass of interlaced fleshy roots. In dividing such roots there is necessarily much waste. Other kinds lend themselves to division much more easily. A few varieties have a way of growing in separate pieces, each piece with a small crown of its own, a characteristic which prevents the development of a fine large plant.

The condition and shape of the roots is influenced by the soil in which they have grown. A deep and friable soil will produce straighter roots than a shallow soil underlain with a hard subsoil. One grower of peonies in England states that he has found peony roots in his garden extending down to a distance of three feet. Exploring roots in their search for food are

forced to turn and twist when they meet an unyielding subsoil.

Before lifting the roots which are to be divided, the leaves and stems should be cut off to the ground. This prevents the rapid softening of the roots, a shock to the plant from which it must recover before it starts to grow again. The soil should be removed and the roots divided with a sharp knife into pieces containing from three to five strong buds or eyes, with a generous proportion of fleshy root. I find that a hunting knife with a six-inch blade is safe to use and has the requisite strength for the work.

Scarce and valuable kinds are cut into smaller pieces so that only one bud is allotted to each piece. If such a fine division is made the new plant should be placed in a cold frame for the first year, as much to keep track of the valuable root as to protect it: such procedure, however, is not an absolute necessity.

One should be warned against too minute or too frequent division. Roots so divided seem to lose their vitality: it may be a long time before they bloom, if they do not succumb entirely.

If in the work of dividing roots of fine varieties some of the fleshy pieces are broken off near the crown, it is well worth while to save them. The upper part of a fleshy root or "finger" will often develop buds and form a crown of its own. The chance of the lower part of a root finger making any growth is very small.

After the roots are cut up the divisions should be planted at once;[1] but, if possible, not in the same soil in which peonies have already been grown. Emphasis should be laid upon this point. Such planting is often, although not invariably, the cause of failure and disappointment. As peonies require much nourishment, they exhaust to an unusual degree the soil in which they grow. If placed in exhausted soil, the new root, suffering from the shock of division and transplanting, is at a great disadvantage: many so planted have failed ever to bloom.

A peony should not be planted in ground that has been previously occupied by one that was diseased.

If it is necessary for the sake of garden design or effect to place a peony where one was growing before, the soil can be entirely removed to a depth of two and a half feet and replaced with fresh soil.

---

1. One prominent grower has recently tried the method of placing the newly divided roots, lightly covered with paper, in a cool, dark place for a day or two and letting the cuts become somewhat callous before replanting. His object in doing this is to lessen the possible danger of rotting.

Raising Peonies from Seed

The growing of peonies from seed is a most fascinating pursuit. As the seedlings are never the same as the parents the possibility of new and more beautiful varieties is a constant hope and a glowing enticement. This possibility appeals strongly to the wish to create which exists in every normal human being. The number of yellow peonies or peonies in which yellow is noticeable is very limited. A glorious yellow peony that will hold its colour for more than a few hours is one of the ambitions of a number of peony lovers. Many of the pink peonies would be lovelier had they less of a bluish tinge. Here are tasks for the enthusiastic amateur. And success in accomplishing them can be attained through seedlings alone.

Peony seeds harden rapidly after ripening and when they have once fully dried it is practically impossible to make them germinate in less than two years. Frequently they require even a longer time. In order to avoid the delay caused by this dryness and hardness the seeds must be gathered just as they are turning brown and must be planted immediately. They should be planted about two inches deep in friable loam. The tiny seedlings will usually appear the following Spring, although some of them may be more deliberate. The seeds may be planted successfully either in the open or in boxes which are about six inches deep and which are placed in cold frames. If planted in boxes they should have plenty of air and moisture, and should be given partial shade to prevent drying out. At the end of a year's growth in the box the seedlings should be transplanted. They may be grown in boxes another year if desired, but after the first transplanting they make more rapid growth if planted outdoors. When these new peonies are three or four years old the anxious gardener may reasonably expect them to bloom. Sad to relate, it is seldom that more than one in a thousand of the seedlings approaches the standards of the old and established varieties. The thrill of having grown them blots out this horrid realization for a while. But the cruel fact that seeds pollinated with the casual assistance of bees and other insects generally produce peonies inferior to those which we already have, is becoming widely appreciated. There promises to be a more definite effort to raise only those seeds which are the result of a careful selection of the parents and of hand pollination.

Hand Pollination

Many beautiful peonies which have been developed within the last fifteen years are the result of careful cross-breeding. Although the breeding of

plants is in itself a life study, there is no reason why the amateur may not, with a little knowledge, enjoy some of its delights and rewards.

The first thing for the novice to learn is the construction of the flower which he wishes to breed. A flower is usually composed of two sets of organs—the non-essential and the essential. The non-essential are (1) the calyx or green cup at the base of the flower, composed of sepals, and (2) the corolla, composed of petals. The essential organs are (3) the pistil and (4) the stamens. The pistil has three parts, the stigma, on which the pollen or fertilising dust is placed, the ovary, which contains the seeds, and the style or slender tube which carries the pollen from the stigma to the ovary. The peony has a compound pistil, the component parts of which are called carpels. Each carpel is composed of a single cell containing many seeds, and the style or extension of the ovary. A groove runs along the inner side of the carpel. This groove contains tiny stigmatic nodules or protuberances.

Both pistil and stamens are to be found in the peony. The stamens, which are usually numerous, surround the pistil. In peonies which have entered into the process of doubling, the stamens may be found amongst the petals throughout the flower. The stamens are in two parts: (1) the anthers or cells full of yellowish powder or pollen, and (2) the filaments or slender stems supporting the anthers. The anthers are composed of two long, narrow cells which open when the pollen is ripe.

Cross-breeding or cross-pollination consists of securing the fertilisation of the seed cells of one peony by placing upon the nodule-covered groove of the carpels the pollen obtained from the anthers of another peony.

The two flowers which have been selected for cross-breeding should be carefully protected to avoid other pollination than that desired. For this purpose oiled paper bags may be placed over the flowers and secured with wire or string. The anthers on the flower which is to be pollinated should be removed as soon as possible, in order to prevent self-fertilisation. Every care should be exercised in removing the anthers to avoid cutting or bruising the carpels. Some of the petals may be removed to facilitate the work. The stigmas should be watched to observe when they are ready to receive the pollen. When the stigmas present a waxy granulated surface they are ready. The pollen should then be taken from the anthers of the pollen parent flower and applied to the receptive stigmas. This may be done in a number of ways. The ripe anther may be crushed upon the thumb nail of the operator or upon a watch crystal or other small receptacle. By means of a tiny scalpel, camel's-hair brush or the operator's finger tips the pollen may then be placed upon the stigmas, which should

be covered generously. Opinions differ as to whether the paper bag should or should not be replaced after the operation is finished. In case the bag is replaced, it should be left only until the stigmas have withered. A tag bearing the names of the parent varieties (the name of the ovule parent appearing first in order) should be securely fastened to the stem.

In crossing some varieties there often arises the difficulty of finding both stigmas and anthers ready for breeding at the same time. Ripe pollen may be kept in dry, air-tight paper bags for a week or more, but the fresher the pollen the more vitality it has. A peony may be forced by planting it in a frame, keeping from frost all Winter, and in the early Spring placing under sash. Forcing in a greenhouse may also be employed.

The equipment for cross-breeding should include a strong magnifying glass, a pair of fine long-handled scissors, a scalpel or a camel's-hair brush and a small receptacle for holding the pollen. Some hybridisers use a jeweller's eyeglass.

Single and semi-double varieties of peonies produce seeds most freely. Full double varieties seldom bear any seeds. In cross-breeding peonies, those two varieties which present most nearly the desired characteristics should be chosen, for in cross-breeding between varieties lies the means of strengthening a type and producing variations. Breeding between individual flowers on the same plant generally produces nothing of value.

The Tree Peony—Description and History

P. MOUTAN—the tree peony—differs from the herbaceous peony in having woody stems that do not die down to the ground in the Autumn. This is the most noticeable structural difference. The leaves are dissimilar in outline from and are usually of a paler shade of green than those of the herbaceous peony (albiflora type). The buds are much larger and flatter and are raised to a sharp point in the centre. They lack any honey secretion and are of the same colour as the leaves.

The tree peony is like the herbaceous in that its flowers have both single and double forms. The flowers of the tree peony, however, usually attain a larger size.

While the tree peony has much in common with the herbaceous peony, it has so much that is distinct that I have thought best to treat it separately. The tree peony has a more extended history and wider cultivation in the Orient than the herbaceous kinds: in Europe and America the reverse is the case.

THE TREE PEONY IN CHINA

In the Sixth Century, A.D., the Chinese distinguished two kinds of peonies—the Mow Tan,[1] or improved kind, the present P. moutan, and the Sho Yo, or common kind, the ancestors or one of the ancestors of the present P. albiflora. The Mow Tans, the more beautiful of the two, were called Hwa Wang—The King of Flowers—and the Sho Yo were called Hwa Leang—The Ministers of the King.

A Chinese author, writing in 536 A.D., says that the original native country of the moutan was the eastern part of the province of Sze-Chuan and

---

1. Mow Tan means "male scarlet flower." It was so called "because of its propagation being principally effected by dividing the root and because the scarlet flower was considered the principal one." The moutan was also known as Muh Sho Yo—"tree-like most beautiful."

the adjacent southern part of the province of Shen-Si (western China—centre—about the latitude of South Carolina). In 656, this statement was corroborated—or copied and accepted as true—by a Chinese writer on natural philosophy.

Prior to 600, the peony was used by the Chinese chiefly for medicinal purposes. About this date, during the reign of the Emperor Yang Te—connoisseur in many things—the tree peony was introduced into gardens as an ornamental plant. By 700, according to an old Chinese work on "The Origin of Things and Matters," the number of sorts grown had greatly increased and the plant was found near the huts of the poor as well as around the houses of the rich. Soon after this, the growing of peonies had become so important that Gow Yang Sew established a genealogical register (Mow tan poo) in which to record the parentage and characteristics of the kinds that were grown from seed. The first botanical garden recorded in history goes back to the time of Queen Hatasu in Egypt, about 1500 B.C. (the Garden of Eden, though doubtless complete in the varieties of the time, did not, so far as we know, include any scheme of classification); but this Chinese pedigree book is the earliest instance I have found of a common or garden tree having a family tree of its own. Thirty different peonies were described under names that allude to their origin or colour or are the names of distinguished persons.

During the Tang Dynasty (618–906 A.D.) the peony acquired an extraordinary fashion and commanded extremely high prices. Poets began to write about it and emperors placed it under their protection. The fields where it was grown were consecrated by inscriptions of a religious enthusiasm. Its culture was the favourite amusement of the nobility, the literary and the rich. Some varieties were held far above the ordinary rates of barter: one kind, called Pe-Leang-Kin—one hundred ounces of gold—and sold for that amount, gives one an idea to what extent the passion for the peony went. Some were regarded as heirlooms; and not infrequently a prize plant was offered as a portion of the marriage dowry.

When the Emperor Yong-Lo of the Ming Dynasty moved the court to Pekin at the end of the Fourteenth Century, he commanded that peonies be brought each year from How-Kow-ang. On their arrival a solemn presentation was held. This ceremony was continued for several centuries.

The tree peonies grown in China were white, pink, red, lilac and, it is stated by some writers, yellow. The wish for a yellow peony has been present in the heart of man for many hundred years. So great was the desire of the Chinese for this colour that they employed many schemes to

procure it: dyes were poured on the roots and white flowers were wrapped in yellow paper with the hope that the petals would take up the colour.

Peonies were grown in the natural shape of bushes, or were trained on espaliers in various designs. Through careful retarding or forcing, they were made to bloom in summer and autumn as well as in the spring.

In the art and literature of China the tree peony has held a conspicuous place. In ceramics, textile and pictorial art and in poetry and prose the peony was an honoured motive or subject. The beauty of the colour and form of the flower has during many centuries made an irresistible appeal to the most cultured inhabitants of the Flowery Kingdom.

In Chinese art, each of the twelve months of the year was represented by a flower—plum for January, peach for February, tree peony for March, double cherry for April, magnolia for May, pomegranate for June, lotus for July, pear for August, mallow for September, chrysanthemum for October, gardenia for November and poppy for December. From the three flowers for the months of each season, one was selected as emblematical of the entire season—the tree peony for Spring, the lotus for Summer, the chrysanthemum for Autumn and the plum for Winter. These four appear as the favourite flowers in all the different forms of Chinese art. They are frequently used in ceramics, particularly in the decoration of the four faces of a quadrangular vase or the four side panels of a bowl. In the patterns of velvets, brocades and woven silks they occur again and again.

Phœnixes, pheasants and peacocks are often depicted with the peony as are storks with the pine, swallows with the willow and quail with millet. It was considered appropriate that the phœnix, the king of all the birds, should appear with the peony, the king of all the flowers. This combination was embroidered with exquisite skill on articles of the trousseaux of the imperial princesses.

In some instances a cock is shown with the peony—the association being based on the fact that both had been held in high regard from the earliest times. The lion—a favourite subject of Chinese ceramic art—is usually pictured with elaborately curled and dressed mane, disporting joyously among peony flowers: apparently even the animals in those days appreciated peonies.

In the Han Period (206 B.C.–220 A.D.), when all the arts were still in their infancy, I find no decorations of peonies on pottery. In the crude bas-reliefs of the time, there are birds which are unmistakably phœnixes and trees or flowers which by a slight exercise of the imagination may be considered

peonies. The bas-relief of the family of Wu at Shantung, 147 A.D., is an example.

In the Sung Period (960–1279 A.D.), among the molded designs used in ceramics were phœnixes flying among peonies. Brocaded patterns composed of interlacing sprays of tree peonies and lilies often occur. A spray of lotus or peony was sometimes engraved under the glaze of dishes.

In the Ming Period (1368–1644 A.D.), when Chinese pottery and porcelain reached a high period of development, the peony was well represented in numerous pieces which were decorated in colour.

In the advance in ceramic art which culminated in the Kang Hsi Period (1662–1796 A.D.), the peony was used more and more frequently as a theme and was portrayed with greater beauty and fidelity. To show the peony as it appears on what is generally considered to be the most wonderful porcelain the world has ever seen, I have reproduced in colour a vase of this period. The vase is one of the Altman collection and has a value of many thousand dollars.

THE TREE PEONY IN JAPAN

About the time of the establishing of the genealogical register in China, many tree peonies were taken to Japan. Under the name Botan (probably the same word as moutan), they at once became great favourites as ornamental plants—a popularity that has continued to the present time. The medicinal qualities of the plant were soon known to the Japanese and in time the culture of the tree peony for sale as a remedy grew into a considerable industry. The provinces of Yomato and Yamasiro (about the same latitude as, but much nearer the sea than, Shen-si—the moutan's original habitat) furnished the market with large quantities of bark and roots. The drug made from the peony apparently does not possess the same fascination as a dispeller of care or a producer of joy as opium or hasheesh: smoking or taking it has never become a national vice in either China or Japan.

The district of Nara in Yomato was famous for its magnificent flowering plants, some of which brought as much as fifty dollars apiece. The best specimens came from the districts near Tokio and Yokohama, where the colder climate produced flowers that had better colour and substance.

The tree peony was the subject of much patient care and clever experimenting. About 1700 A.D., Ito Ifui, a Japanese gardener, agile with both spade and pen, wrote detailed and extended instructions for the culture of the tree peony which included propagating from cuttings and some methods of grafting.

The Japanese take a pride in the tree peony that is second only to that taken in the chrysanthemum. On the eighty-eighth day after January first the Japanese farmer starts his agricultural operations for the year. Shortly after this important event the tree peony comes into bloom and flower shows for it are held over the entire country. In some of these exhibitions as many as five thousand plants of varying colours are arranged in tier upon tier of brilliancy.

The tree peony is classed with the iris, lotus and wistaria as the most important flowers of summer. The peony, the cherry and the lotus are the three flowers to which is attributed royal rank. The tree peony was often called the Flower of Prosperity and occasionally the Plant of Twenty Days, because of the long time during which the flowers preserved their beauty and freshness.

The tree peony and chrysanthemum are not used in the landscape garden proper. Their display is restricted to flower beds arranged in long sheltered areas which are usually placed near the apartments of the ladies. In the grounds of the palaces peonies adorn the open spaces facing the ladies' chambers from which the beauty of the flowers can be readily viewed.

The peony was much cherished by the upper classes, who gave it "scrupulous care and nursing" in order to produce flowers of enormous size. This care included, according to Ito Ifui, the rubbing of the stems with camellia oil in order to free the bark of lichens and moss!

In Japanese art the plum blossom is inseparably connected with the nightingale. Similar combinations of bird and flower or beast and flower are found in the many designs of the country, as, for example, bamboo leaves and sparrows, deer and maple leaves, peonies and peafowl.

The "exuberant flower" of the peony, with its long, curling petals, was a favourite subject in art. With peacock or Shishi—a kind of conventional lion derived from the Chinese—the peony forms the constant decoration of temple and palace walls.

As the peony was given royal rank and was regarded as the queen of all flowering plants, it had to be used alone in any indoor flower arrangement and had to be placed in the position of honour in the room, that is, on the dais of the principal recess.

The peony has a place in the religion of the Japanese. In Shintoism, there is a festival called Bommatsuri, celebrated on July 13–15 in each year, which corresponds to our All Saints' Day. At this time departed spirits return for a brief earthly sojourn. Elaborate ceremonies are held in each house. Choice dishes are prepared and at night the way is lighted for the

spirits by persons carrying "peony lanterns," which consist of candles fastened in the centre of artificial peonies made of paper or silk and swung by a fine wire bale on the end of a long pole.[2]

The affection of the Japanese people for the peony is shown by the numerous legends and bits of folk-lore concerning it, all of which are marked by a charming symbolism. In many of these the soul of the peony inhabits a body which is apparently human, but which suddenly disappears on sufficient provocation. In one legend, a Japanese scholar made the cultivation of peonies his sole recreation. On a sunny morning a beautiful woman clothed in purest white appeared at his door, and asked permission to become a member of his household. On account of her loveliness the request was granted. For days, contented and happy, she joined in tending the treasured peonies. During a terrible storm, a dark, mysterious stranger sought shelter in the house. On seeing him the woman ran in fear. When the scholar followed her she fell to the ground, apparently in a swoon; he stooped to lift her, but she faded before his very eyes and vanished. She was the Spirit of the Peony. When next the scholar went into the garden he found that all his peonies had been destroyed by the rain.

THE TREE PEONY IN ENGLAND

Although known in England in 1669 nothing was done to import the tree peony into that country until the latter part of the Nineteenth Century. From Chinese drawings and from praises bestowed on the plant in books, an "ardent desire was excited in Sir Joseph Banks—the head of the Royal Botanical Gardens at Kew—and others to obtain some of the plants." In 1786 Sir Joseph commissioned Mr. Duncan—"a medical gentleman attached to the East India Company's service"—to procure a plant for Kew. This was done and the first tree peony in England was seen at the Royal Garden in 1787. The plant P. Banksii, which had flesh pink double flowers, and several others which were received from time to time, uniformly failed to thrive—due probably, as one English writer surmises, to being too rapidly forced as "stove" plants.

In 1794 a fresh supply of tree peonies was purchased in Canton and sent to England. Owing to the long voyage and improper packing, many of these died en route: only three plants survived the trip. On arrival at Kew, the three were successfully grown outdoors, propagated, and distributed

---

2. Lafcadio Hearn described another kind of peony lantern made by attaching to the top of a festival lantern artificial peonies of silk.

in British collections. These peonies had deep pink flowers and were named Rosea. Later many other importations were made consisting of the above varieties and the Papaveracea or poppy-flowered peony. For a time high prices were paid for the plants.

In 1838, a monograph on the peony describes only the tree peonies I have mentioned, but in 1850 there were a dozen distinct kinds in cultivation in England. Some of these had probably been raised from seed obtained from the three original varieties imported. The Earl of Mount Morris and the Earl of Sandwich both took a great interest in the tree peony and produced several distinct sorts from the Papaveracea.

In 1860 the English gardens were chiefly supplied by French growers. In the English magazines of the eighties there are references to "Whitsun roses," which was the popular name by which the tree peony was then known to the trade.

For some time past, the English appear to have wanted a blue peony above all others. In about 1875 this colour is referred to as being the most highly desired. In 1880, Robert Fortune was commissioned by the Royal Horticultural Society to find a blue peony. After much searching in China, he succeeded in finding a moutan with lilac flowers—which seems to be the nearest to the ideal yet realized.

About 1870 an English nurseryman collected seeds of all the varieties in commerce and started propagation of tree peonies. These plants have gradually been grown by more and more persons. In 1890 it was said that the sorts offered could be counted by the hundreds. At the present time English growers list no less than one hundred and ten different kinds.

Although there are numerous instances of tree peonies not thriving in England, they are cultivated successfully in many parts of that country. Failure to grow well has probably been due to local conditions.

I find the mention of one tree peony in England in 1835 that "perfected" 320 flowers in one season. There are statements here and there about occasional specimens noted for their huge size and their abundance of bloom. One plant in particular, grown in the garden of E. Taylor, Diss, Norfolk, is famous for its long life and sturdy growth. In 1904, when eighty years old, it was fifteen feet across and produced 400 flowers from eight to nine inches in diameter.

It is stated by one writer that the "re-introduction" of the tree peony in England was mainly due to T. S. Ware of Tottenham, whose display of the flowers was always a great feature.

THE TREE PEONY IN AMERICA

We have no exact knowledge as to the date when the tree peony was introduced into the United States. Hovey (writing in 1836) thinks it must have been about 1820. In 1826, a plant of P. moutan, var. papavaracea, was imported from England by William Lathe of Cambridgeport—probably a wise and public-spirited move, for if ever a place (from its present appearance) needed brightening up it must have been Cambridgeport.[3]

In 1828 the catalogue of John Bartram lists the same variety, adding "poppy flowered tree pæony," but without price, and "P. moutan rosea, rose coloured," at five dollars. William Prince's catalogue for the following year for the Linnæan Botanic Garden at Flushing, Long Island, sets out these varieties and also P. moutan Banksi "Chinese purple tree pæony with magnificent fragrant flowers," all at five dollars apiece. So even in the days when the high cost of living was not a vital issue tree peonies were not an inexpensive hobby.

In 1836 Colonel Perkins of Brookline, Massachusetts, imported direct from China a tree peony, which was thought to have been P. moutan Rawsei. At the same date a Mr. Wilder of Dorchester is recorded as the owner of several of the latest seedlings which he had received from France.

In 1862, Prince, at great trouble and expense, obtained some twenty varieties of tree peonies from European gardens and introduced them at Flushing. He says, in that year: "I have also originated from seeds during the past fifteen years twenty-two most gorgeous varieties, whose flowers are of the largest size, and comprising white, roseate, crimson, lilac, purple and variegated shades."

At the present time there are a few gardens in this country in which the tree peony is made an important feature. It is not, however, grown in the United States nearly as widely as in England and France. Its charms are not well known to the gardener, it does not make the same sentimental appeal that the herbaceous peony does, and it is not offered so freely by the nurseries. Some houses do not list it at all, others sparingly. As an example two large growers of herbaceous peonies each catalogue less than a dozen varieties of P. moutan. As the plant has such wonderful beauty and such an interesting historical background, more discriminating amateurs will, as time goes on, probably come to include it among their cherished floral treasures.[4]

---

3. It is an historical fact that this peony was later moved from Cambridgeport to the place of J. P. Cushing, Watertown, Mass.
4. Since the above was written, Mr. B. H. Farr has imported a collection of over two thousand tree peonies, which will undoubtedly be the beginning here of a wider acquaintance with this beautiful plant.

Tree Peonies: Cultivation, Propagation and Best Varieties

LOCATION AND SOIL

IN growing tree peonies, location and soil are important. The tree peony should always be planted at a distance from trees or shrubs and sheltered from the north and east winds. A friable and rich vegetable garden soil, similar to that which should be provided for herbaceous peonies, is best. If the ground is poor it should be made fertile by the addition of well-rotted manure or compost. . . . Observant gardeners have noticed that soils in which there is considerable iron are particularly suited to growing tree peonies. Where the iron is deficient, the application of a small quantity—preferably in the form of the sulphate—is of value in producing vigour in the plant and depth of colour in the blooms.

In addition to proper location and good soil, drainage is most necessary: excessive moisture encourages the development of a white fungus to which the tree peony is susceptible.

PLANTING

Late September or early October is the best time for planting tree peonies. The roots should always be closely examined for white fungus. Any rotted parts should be cut off, and the roots given a soaking in a five per cent solution of formalin. Unless the fungus is thoroughly removed it will spread and eventually cause the death of the peony. In planting, care should be taken that the roots do not cross each other, and that the tree is set at the same depth as it was in the nursery.

CULTIVATION

Tree peonies, unlike herbaceous peonies, should never be cut down. With the exception of an occasional shaping of the tree and the removal of the ends of the branches when they have died back a little, pruning is unnecessary.

For the first winter after planting the ground should be mulched with a light covering so that the roots will not heave as a result of frost. Each Autumn, in order to prevent the breaking of the branches by heavy snows and to help protect the trees from the unscrupulous appetites of hungry rabbits, I tie up my tree peonies with straw in a manner similar to that in which roses are generally prepared for Winter. After the first warm days of Spring have brought life into the buds of P. moutan, late frosts often do much damage. For this reason I never remove the straw in early Spring. The binding strings are cut and the straw is loosely woven through the branches or drawn up tent-wise and tied to a tall stake so as to keep off the cold sweeping winds of April and the sudden still frosts. If by any mischance the buds should be nipped, they should be shaded from the sun at once and allowed to thaw gradually. Such a misfortune has never occurred in my own garden: the use of the loose straw in the branches has always proved effective. Contrary to expectation, the straw covering does not hasten the Spring growth of the peonies, and so does no harm. A small frame covered with muslin or canvas has been suggested as another simple and practical method of protection from late frosts.

The tree peony will, under favorable conditions, live a great many years. There are records of some ninety years old. When once established they should be left undisturbed indefinitely.

FERTILISING

The tree peony may be fertilised in the same manner as the herbaceous. In moderation, weak manure water, wood ashes and bone meal may all be safely used. The Japanese successfully employ a special mixture composed as follows:

> Compost $1\frac{1}{2}$–$1\frac{3}{4}$ lbs.
> Superphosphate of lime $\frac{1}{2}$ oz.
> Straw ash 2–3 oz.
> Oil cake $\frac{1}{2}$ lb.
> Saltpetre $\frac{1}{2}$ oz.

This formula was recently given to me by a larger grower of tree peonies in Japan, and as the culture of the tree peony receives especial care in that country, the information should be valuable. Like all other fertilisers, the mixture must be used with extreme caution.

Fertilisers may be applied to the best advantage at any one of the following times: one month after the flowering is over, in the Autumn after the leaves fall, in the Spring before the buds start forth, or just before the flowers open.

It would be of interest to know what methods the Chinese gardeners use in cultivating the famous tree peonies in the gardens of the Mandarins, where the plants frequently attain great size and produce as many as three or four hundred flowers every year. There is little material available on the subject of Chinese gardens and gardening, and the Chinese themselves seem indisposed to enlighten us. There are no exporting nurseries in China and the difficulties of obtaining either peonies or facts as to culture are almost insurmountable.

FORCING

Tree peonies lend themselves most willingly to the process of forcing, provided it is gentle and applied to good, strong plants. They should be taken first into a house that is slightly heated, say 40°–50° F. In about two weeks, or as soon as the buds begin to swell, the peonies may be removed to a temperature of about 55° F., where they will flower in five or six weeks. Frequent watering is necessary and if the atmosphere is dry the plants should be sprayed in addition to the watering. As soon as the flowers open, water should be applied to the roots only. The flowering season will be quite long if the tree is strong and has set many buds. After forcing, tree peonies require two or three years for recuperation. Because the blooms of double-flowered varieties last longer upon the plant, those varieties are best for forcing. Reine Elizabeth, Lactea, Jules Pirlot and Lord Macartnay are excellent for this purpose.

PROPAGATION

GRAFTING

The usual method of propagating tree peonies is by grafting. In China and in France they are grafted upon the fleshy roots of herbaceous peonies. In

Japan the practice is to graft upon the wild moutan stock, but this is far from satisfactory. The wild moutan stock is so strong and persistent that a constant struggle is necessary to prevent the graft from being choked out. The graft sometimes makes roots of its own and thus becomes established, but it is at the price of eternal vigilance on the gardener's part. At the present time I know of but one grower who imports the Japanese varieties and who grafts them upon herbaceous roots.

The method of grafting known in China since about 1000 A.D., and followed there and in France, and also in this country by some enthusiasts who grow tree peonies, is the best. Seeds of herbaceous peonies—P. albiflora—are sown in large quantities to furnish roots. A good piece of root, about the size of one's middle finger, is selected and slit from the crown downwards for about two inches. The scion from the tree peony should have at least two eyes. It is cut in the shape of a wedge and after being fitted with exactness into the slit, is bound in the usual way. The grafted root is placed in a deep pot of soil, with one eye of the moutan scion below the surface. The pot is then placed in a frame.

The grafting should be done in August or September so that the stock will develop roots before the Winter. After a season's growth in the cold frame the peony may be planted out and cultivated the same as an established plant. In this way the tree peony in time develops its own roots, and does not cause annoyance by suckering.

LAYERING

A number of other methods have been used for propagating tree peonies. Of these, layering is perhaps the simplest. Year-old shoots of a strong, healthy plant are firmly pegged down in the Autumn. The first year after pegging, roots are thrown out from each bud, and the second year the new little plants are removed from the parent tree.

DIVISION

Division of the roots to increase any especially desirable kinds has also been employed. This is done during the Autumn, at the usual planting time. In dividing the roots care is taken that each division retains some fibrous rootlets. I do not know to just what extent this method is practised. It would seem to have the serious drawback of destroying a well-established plant and taking great risks with the success of the divisions. Grafting upon herbaceous roots has proved to be the most practical and successful method of increasing the stock of existing varieties.

SEEDS

The planting of the seeds of tree peonies, as is the case with herbaceous peonies, brings new varieties into existence. There is a constant surprise and delight in raising tree peonies from seed: beautiful and wonderful flowers reward the patient gardener. Patience is indeed necessary. The seeds, if planted as soon as they become ripe, take at least a year to germinate—and a much longer time if they have been allowed to become dry and hard before being planted. After the little plants appear, from five to seven years must pass before one can hope for flowers. But during the long wait when the plants are still too young to bloom they have a charm of their own in the diversity of their foliage. I know of two gardens where tree peony seeds are planted regularly each year, so that there are new ones blooming every season.

Tree peonies raised from seeds have the great advantage of being on their own roots from the start. Then, too, the seedlings, although differing from the parents in most instances, equal them in beauty. This is a point worthy of consideration: for the same difficulty exists in purchasing Japanese tree peonies true to name and description as is the case with the Japanese herbaceous varieties.

In Chapter 7 directions are given for the planting and cultivation of herbaceous peony seeds. The same directions may be followed in the care of the seeds and little plants of P. moutan.

BEST VARIETIES

The tree peony deserves a much wider appreciation and cultivation in this country than it now receives. While its requirements are more exacting than those of the herbaceous peony, it is far from being as fragile and difficult to grow as is often supposed, and is more worth while than other plants on which it is necessary to expend greater care.

In addition to the European varieties of tree peony mentioned in Chapter 4, and the varieties especially good for forcing mentioned above, I append a list of twelve beautiful tree peonies which also are European—not Japanese. Some of these varieties can be bought in this country. All can be obtained from French growers.

FRAGRANS MAXIMA PLENA, flesh pink and salmon.

GLOBOSA, very full, white with red splashes.

GLORY OF SHANGHAI, anemone type. Glossy bright pink.

JEANNE D'ARC, very large, full flower. Salmon pink with yellow tints.

LAMBERTINÆ, white, shaded with pink and purple.

LOUISE MOUCHELET, very large, double, salmon flesh pink.

MADAME LAFFAY, large full bloom, violet, rose and white.

ROBERT FORTUNE, brilliant salmon red, fringed petals.

SAMARANG, semi-double, bright scarlet, black spots.

SOUVENIR DE DUCHER, full globular flowers, deep violet with reddish tinge.

SOUVENIR DE MADAME KNORR, large, double, pale flesh-pink splashed with purple.

VILLE DE SAINT DENIS, very large white flower, tinted purple.

CHAPTER TEN

Various Species of the Peony

T HE peony belongs to the order Ranunculaceæ (from rana, a frog, because certain members of the family thrive in swampy places). The order—sometimes called Crowfoot—embraces twenty-seven genera of plants, including such familiar friends as Aconites, Anemones, Buttercups, Clematis, Columbines, Fennels, Hellebores and Larkspurs.

There are between eighteen and twenty-five species of the Genus Pæonia. Few botanists agree as to the exact number or as to the status of many of the varieties. This is not surprising, for in the herbarium different species are often almost indistinguishable and in the garden a certain number vary by characters of most unequal value.

A key to the species of the Genus Pæonia was worked out by Dr. Coit in 1907, based on earlier descriptions. While this key is not final it is a great assistance in making classifications. In view of recent information, I have made some changes in this table and reprint it on page 104.

For the benefit of those who may wish to start collecting peonies of botanical or historical interest, or who may wish to use some of the wild species in hybridising, I give a few notes on a number of species and some of their varieties, which notes include the original habitat and a short description of the flower.[1]

1.   Albiflora (white flowered). Central China and Siberia.
     Older Varieties:
         Candida.
         Festiva.
         Fragrans.
             The first named albiflora to be imported into England (1805).
         Humei.
         Pottsii.

---

1. For complete botanical descriptions of the principal varieties, see Bailey's Standard Cyclopedia of Horticulture, Vol. III, p. 2431 (1916).

Introduced in 1821, from China, by John Potts, a collector who had been sent there by the Royal Horticultural Society. There are six peonies named Pottsii or a variety of the same. The famous Pottsii in John Richardson's garden was a rich deep crimson and double.

Reevesii.

Introduced from China by John Reeves. Flowers dark red with slight magenta tint.

Rubescens.

Vestalis.

Whitleyi.

Introduced in 1808.

More Recent Varieties:

See Main List of Peonies, Chapter 3.

2. Anomala (unusual—referring to the leaves, which are finely divided). Siberia.

Stated by some writers to be the same as P. Emodi, which it very evidently is not. First mentioned in Flora Siberica (St. Petersburg, 1747.) Flowers with irregular petals of a brilliant red and with clusters of yellow stamens. The roots grow to great size and are used by the Mongol Tartars for food.

Varieties:

Insignis (remarkable).

A form of this is grown in gardens under the name of Peter Barr. Flowers magenta.

Intermedia (intermediate).

Flowers rosy crimson.

3. Arietina (ram's horn fruited). Levant and Crete.

It is a very early bloomer. Index Kewensis regards this as a form of peregrina. Flowers dark red; each leaf is divided into segments, each from one to two inches wide.

4. Brownii (Brown's). California and Northwest.

This is the only species native to the Western Hemisphere. It blooms in June and July, often near banks of melting snow. The flowers are dull red or brown and are not attractive.

5. Cambessedesii (Cambessedes's). Balearic Islands and Corsica.

Flowers deep rose pink with slight magenta tint. Introduced into England in 1896 by Miss F. Geoghegan.

6. Corallina (coral-red, referring to the seeds). Southern Europe to Asia Minor.

> It is claimed that Corallina has grown wild on an island in the Severn. If this is true, it is the only peony native to England. Flowers, bright crimson. The segments of the leaves are quite distinct from one another at the base and nine in number in the fully developed lowest leaves.

Varieties:

> Broteri (Brotero's).
>
> Spain and Portugal. Dwarf habit, flowers crimson, stems and leaf-stalks red.
>
> Fragrant.
>
> This variety is probably the P. Lusitanica of Philip Miller.
>
> Russi (Russ's). Corsica, Sardinia, Algeria.
>
> Flowers rose coloured.
>
> Triternata (three times ternate, *i.e.*, with twenty-seven leaflets).
>
> Rose and whitish flowers.

7. Coriacea (leathery). Spain, North Africa.

> Flowers bright crimson, seeds dark purple. Leaves composed of nine to thirteen leaflets, which become leathery as they advance in age.

8. Decora (comely).

> The first mention of this peony is that seeds came from Constantinople. Flowers rather small, dark red, tinted magenta. Dwarf habit, very bushy.

Varieties:

> Alba (white).
>
> Satiny white, tinted pink.
>
> Elatior (taller).
>
> Large magenta coloured flowers.
>
> Pallasii (Pallass's—originally Byzantina).
>
> Deep crimson flowers.

9. Delavayi (Delavay's). China.

> Woody stems, small flowers, red, tinted magenta.

Variety:

> Angustiloba (narrow-leaved).
>
> Finely divided leaves.

10. Emodi (Mount Emodus—not found in modern gazetteers).

> This is the only peony native to India. It grows in the temperate

zone in the Himalayan Mountains from Kumaon to Kashmir. Flowers single, four to six inches across, pure white with prominent yellow stamens. One of the most beautiful of the single flowers. The plant has a slender growth and a distinctive habit. Although more tender than any other herbaceous variety, it is one of the wild varieties worth growing in the garden. Index Kewensis considers this a form of P. anomala. Other authorities state that it is closely allied to P. albiflora, with which (and Veitchii) it shares the unusual characteristic of bearing more than one flower on a stem. Of the one to five flowers which grow on a stem rarely more than two are in bloom at the same time.

11. Lutea (yellow)—see page 62.

  Variety:

    Superba.

    Large flowers.

12. Mlokosewitschii. Eastern part of the central Caucasus.

  Discovered by Mlokosewitsch and only recently introduced. Single flowers of sulphur yellow. Leaves have red veins and margins. Probably closely related to Wittmaniana.

13. Moutan—see Suffruticosa below.

14. Obovata (obovate—referring to the petals). Siberia, Manchuria, China.

  Introduced into England in 1900 by E. H. Wilson, who sent seeds collected in the Province of Hupeh, central China. Flowers purplish red; seeds like berries, dark blue.

15. Officinalis (of the apothecary shops)—see page 61.

  Varieties:

    Albicans.

    Old double white, which opens a pale flesh and gradually changes to a pure white.

    Anemoneflora.

    Single and double crimson with magenta tint.

    Blanda (alluring).

    Pale purple—unlike its name, not desirable.

    Carnescens.

    Deep rose coloured, which grows paler after opening. Sometimes called variegated peony.

    Lobata.

    A dwarf form.

Rubra.

Brilliant red—the common red peony.

Rosea.

Rose coloured.

Sabini.

Single red, yellow stamens and anthers.

16. Paradoxa (paradoxical). Levant.

First cultivated in Holland. One of the smallest peonies. Bright carmine pink flowers on very short stems. Lower leaves finely divided.

Variety:

Fimbriata (fringed).

Semi-double flowers of bright crimson, inner ones narrow like a fringe.

17. Peregrina (foreign). Southern Europe.

Flowers are deep red. Lower leaves finely divided.

Varieties:

Humilis (dwarf), mountains of Spain.

Bright red flowers, turning to magenta.

Microcarpa (small fruited).

Even smaller than Humilis, to which it is closely allied.

18. Suffruticosa (woody) or Tree Peony. See page 62.

19. Tenuifolia (slender leaved). See page 60.

Varieties:

Rubra plena (double red).

Latifolia (broad leaved).

20. Veitchii (Veitch's). Western China.

Recently introduced by E. H. Wilson. Flowers purplish crimson; several blooms on one stem.

21. Wittmaniana (Wittman's). Caucasus. See page 60.

A   Plants shrubby; disk enveloping the base of the carpels. .... { *Moutan* / *Lutea* / *Delavayi* }

AA   Plant herbaceous; disk not enveloping the base of the carpels.

    B   Petals short and leathery, scarcely exceeding the sepals. .... *Brownii*

    BB   Petals not leathery, large and expanding, much exceeding the sepals.

      C   Carpels glabrous.

        D   Stems usually several headed. .... { *Albiflora* / *Veitchii* }

        DD   Stems one-headed.

          E   Petals yellow or yellowish. .... { *Wittmaniana* / *Mlokosewitchii* }

          EE   Petals not yellowish.

            F   Leaves glabrous on both sides. .... *Obovata*

            FF   Leaves pubescent beneath.

              G   Corolla red to purple. .... *Corsica*

              GG   Corolla bright crimson. .... *Coriacea*

                H   Calyx with 2 or 3 large foliaceous outer sepals. ......

                HH   Calyx with 1 or 2 large compound leaves from its base. .... *Emodi*

      CC   Carpels tomentose.

        D   Stems usually several headed. ....

        DD   Stems never more than one-headed.

          E   Lfts. finely dissected.

            F   Root tubers fascicled with creeping stolons. .... *Tenuifolia*

            FF   Stolons none. .... *Anomala*

          EE   Lfts. not finely divided.

            F   Carpels erect—arcuate.

              G   Shoots glabrous in upper part, pilose below. ..... *Officinalis*

              GG   Shoots hairy above, glabrous below.

                H   Lfts. 15–20 in number. .... *Peregrina*

                HH   Lfts. 30–40 in number. .... *Paradoxa*

            FF   Carpals wide spreading when mature.

              G   Leaves pubescent beneath.

                H   Stem 2–3 ft. tall, pubescent above. .... *Ariettina*

              GG   Leaves glabrous on both sides. .... { *Decora* / *Corallina* }

Why Some Peonies Do Not Bloom

WITH peonies, as with people, bloom is the expression of health and well-being. If one's peonies do not bear flowers, something is wrong. Perhaps there are several conditions which contribute to their failure. Herbert Spencer truly said that there is no such thing as cause and effect: it is "causes and effects."

Here are the principal reasons why some peonies do not bloom.

1. **Roots reaching the end of a useful existence.** . . . I spoke of the length of life of P. albiflora. Its span of years differs according to the variety, but none of the varieties reaches the great age of either P. officinalis or P. Moutan. The gardener must realize this and be prepared when the time arrives to replace the old plants with young ones.

2. **Transplantation of large roots without division.** Peonies which have grown in one place for over three years will often refuse to bloom if they are moved without being divided. A one-, two-, or three-year root will go on blooming cheerfully, but roots older than three years may easily refuse to flower well again for a considerable period after transplanting. Occasionally even a three-year-old root will sulk. It is a good general rule never to transplant a peony without division, provided it is fit for division. Roots bought from growers are usually already divided quite as much as—or more than!—is good for them, and should not be divided further.

3. **Recent transplantation.** Many peonies will not bloom the first season or two after being planted. These roots demand time in which to settle down to the business of life in their new homes. This is usually the case with varieties which are not naturally profuse bloomers.

4. **Divisions from roots that are too old.** A number of reasons for the failure of such divisions to bloom have already been discussed. . . . It will suffice here to repeat that the badly balanced root-systems which necessarily occur in divisions of old peonies often fail to supply food and moisture to the growing plant. The new-made root has a struggle for life. It has no energy left to expend in flowering.

5. Divisions from weak or overworked stock. As a rule, divisions of new and scarce varieties are too weak to bloom for several years, unless the division has been made in one's own garden with the proper exercise of judgment and care. Certainly the small pieces so often sold by professional growers have a long fight ahead of them, before they acquire sufficient strength to flower. Not only are the pieces tiny, but they are from stock too frequently divided.

A sad letter from a collector, received the very day I am writing these lines, is in point. In 1918 he and another enthusiast bought a division of a rare and expensive variety. It was small when they bought it, but they witlessly proceeded to divide it again so that there might be a piece for each to have and to hold and to plant. Four years have dragged slowly by and it has not yet bloomed. He "hopes" that it will flower this year, but admits that the hope is only a slight one.

It is bad enough to receive stock which has already been often and closely divided, but deliberately to cut it further one's self is really courting disaster.

6. Too deep planting. This may come about by intention or by accident. The places prepared for peony roots are seldom made ready a sufficiently long time in advance to permit the ground to settle thoroughly. Ground that is deeply dug and turned will settle and pack to a surprising degree. How much greater will the settling be when part of the soil is removed in preparation and replaced with compost which by nature is less closely packed! If the root is planted before this settling process is complete, it is naturally carried down with the earth, and even though it has been placed at the proper depth in the first place, it does not stay there. The unsightly depression caused by the sinking is then filled by the gardener, who unthinkingly imprisons the poor root perhaps five or six inches below the surface.

From the gardens of amateurs—advanced to perfection in growing other flowers—peony roots have been brought to me, each one showing two distinct clumps, one above the other. The upper clump has been the result of the peony's efforts for years to struggle up out of its grave. The plants showed plainly that the original crowns had reached a point eight inches below the surface. In whatever way they were buried, whether through too deep planting in the first place or through the constant filling and leveling of the holes, it is not surprising that they never smiled upon the garden.

7. **Improper location.** If the peony is planted in the wrong place, it will have difficulty in producing flowers. In ground that is too dry, flowers will fail. In soil that is too wet or insufficiently drained, the root will rot and blossoms will be lacking. Constant and excessive shade will discourage the most persistent bloomer. It is amazing how many people apparently take pleasure in planting their peonies under big trees, in dry and heavily shaded soil. One sees this often in suburban gardens where space is at a premium. Repeatedly the owners of such plantings ask aggrievedly why their peonies do not bloom. When the damning closeness of the trees is pointed out, the answer is invariably, "Oh—but I can't move my trees, you know!"

8. **Exhausted or infected soil.** The growth of a peony in one place for a number of years exhausts the soil. If after the removal of an old root, another peony is planted in the same place, it is not apt to succeed. The new peony cannot find enough food in the famished soil. And if it is suffering from the shock of division,—which is usually the case,—the effort to become established is doubly difficult. Not only do many peonies fail to thrive under these conditions, but some of them succumb entirely. Naturally, the length of time the ground was previously occupied affects the degree of its poverty. But more and more is becoming recognized the importance of planting peonies in fresh ground—ground that is rich, well cultivated, sweet, and in good heart.

Another reason for always planting peonies in fresh soil is the danger of infection from sick plants. A root suffering from black rot may leave infected bits or fungoid spores in the ground. And if by any chance the former occupant suffered from root-galls, then the presence of depraved nematode worms in the soil approaches a certainty. To subject a new and healthy root to such conditions and expect it to survive and bloom rapturously is asking too much.

In case it is desirable for the sake of garden design to plant a peony where one was grown before, the earth may be removed to a depth of two feet and replaced by fresh topsoil. The new root will then have a fair start.

9. **Late frosts.** Not often in the vicinity of New York is frost a cause of damage to the peony buds. However, last year (1922) a late and bitter frost did great harm, not only in this locality but in many parts of the country. I shall not soon forget the frost which in one night turned the gorgeous magnolias from masses of pink loveliness into brown and heartbreaking disappointments. Some of the French lilac buds were also nipped, and had

my tree peonies not been screened with straw, all of them would have gone. The herbaceous peonies which were planted among peach trees were practically unscathed. While those situated in other places lost some of the terminal buds, many of these injured buds were later replaced by laterals. The crops were so small that the growers of peonies for the cut-flower market suffered great loss, and many a little garden missed its year's display. We are hardened to the possible late freezing of our peaches; but deprivation of our peony blooms is a novel shock.

The heavy frosts, though damaging, are fortunately not frequent. The lighter frosts have never harmed peonies in my garden.

10. Diseased plants. Stalks of peonies which are suffering from "bud blast," one of the symptoms of botrytis, will not bloom. Wilting of the stems and rotting of the buds are other effects of the same disease. Peonies which are afflicted with root-gall bloom uncertainly or not at all.

Information regarding both these diseases will be found in the next chapter.

Diseases of Peonies

I N THE preceding chapter the reasons which are given for the peony's failure to bloom may be called outside causes or circumstances. They are readily remedied by some simple change in the method of cultivation. But more and more does one hear about the inroads of wilt, black rot, bud-blast, and botrytis.

It may be that these troubles do not attack the peony with greater frequency than they did years ago, but as more garden-makers adopt this flower as a special interest, so there will be wider discussion of its ailments as well as its charms. It is certain, however, that these symptoms of fungoid disease, which have now become the subject of careful scientific study, have troubled the peony for many years.

Sunlight and air are destructive to botrytis. Although the culture of peonies in open fields—in large spaces which are well away from infection—is seldom hampered by any of the manifestations of botrytis, still it is sadly true that peonies in gardens are often affected. An old garden, with close planting which shades the ground and with topsoil composed largely of stable manure and vegetable matter, provides conditions favorable to the growth of this fungus.

The horticultural magazines to-day contain many letters and articles on this peony-blight, as it is called. Recently there have appeared strong recommendations to spray both the peonies and the ground in which they are planted.

As long ago as 1911, this suggestion of spraying for the control of this fungus was made by Mr. A. H. Fewkes of Newton Highlands, Massachusetts. He has tried at different times the following treatments: air-slaked lime, dry Bordeaux-mixture, sulpho-naphthol, and "Sulco V. B." (which is made from sulphur, carbolic acid, and fish-oil). Mr. Fewkes avows that the last preparation has a vile odor,—which is not hard to believe,—but that it appears to be doing good work. When a plant shows disease he scrapes away the affected portion of the root and applies the fungicide before fill-

ing in with fresh earth.

In my own garden prevention more than cure has been my dependence. In the first place, my peonies are grown away from other plants. That in itself is a protection. In the second place, the foliage is cut off and removed each fall with scrupulous care; it is then immediately burned, as advised in Chapter 6. Thirdly, the plants are under careful daily observation. All flowers which are not to be saved for seed are cut off and burned as soon as they begin to fade. The occasional dried or undeveloped buds are snipped off with speed, and burned. Seldom do I find wilted or broken stalks. In a season of excessive wet they will occur, but their number is undoubtedly kept down by persistent and prompt inspection. When a stem is found to be affected, it is severed close to the ground. The soil around it is then removed and the sick stalk is followed below the surface down to the root itself, which is then carefully examined without being disturbed any more than is necessary. Fresh earth or sand is brought to replace that which was taken off the root. At the risk of being thought painfully thorough, I will admit that the old soil is well scorched before it is carried away—just to be sure!

In the removal of all these parts—buds, stems, and faded flowers—it is well to work gently, as careless or rough handling will do much to spread the spores.

So far in my experience I have never had to spray my peonies. A light application of water-slaked stone lime to the beds every few years keeps the soil sweet and discourages fungus. Upon the complete withholding of solid manure too much stress cannot be laid; for, while manure encourages a strong growth of plants, it makes the soil in time favorable to the breeding of fungus spores.

The careful burning of both sick and ripe foliage is another vital point. Unflagging attention to these details has so far sufficed to keep my peonies from falling victims to the dreaded botrytis.

Another disease which sometimes troubles the peony is known as root-gall. Peonies affected with this disease have many weak stalks, which are stunted and give no bloom. The roots are short and stubby, with swellings and lumps. The tips of the roots appear to be rotted. The fine rootlets have many small galls or lumps upon them. Root-gall occurs much oftener in the South and in light soils than it does in the North and in heavy soils. In heavy soils the trouble is not usually serious, although individual roots may be beyond cure. A badly infected root had best be burned. A valuable root which is only lightly troubled may frequently be divided and reset in fresh soil. This treatment will often overcome a slight infestation.

The constant replanting of roots upon the same soil is one cause of the spread of this disease. I called attention in Chapter 6 to the importance of planting always upon new soil. This applies to all peonies, either sick or in health. And if the gardener is trying to cure an infected root by frequent division and resetting in fresh soil, as suggested, such planting should, if possible, be carefully kept to itself in a part of the grounds outside of the garden.

Two important and instructive pamphlets upon these diseases have been written. In 1911 the United States Department of Agriculture, through the Bureau of Plant Industry, printed Bulletin No. 217, entitled *Root-Knot and Its Control*. It was written by Professor Ernst A. Bessey. It is of the greatest value, and should be in the library of every serious gardener.

In 1915 Prof. H. H. Whetzel of Ithaca, New York, gave a lecture before the Massachusetts Horticultural Society upon "Diseases of the Peony." This lecture was later printed in pamphlet form. Dr. Whetzel treats at length of botrytis as well as root-gall, and illustrations of the many manifestations of both diseases are added to the clear explanations of the text. This is another publication of immense usefulness, which should be in the possession of good gardeners.

While the various troubles and diseases of the peony are being considered here, I would like to enter protest against the name "Lemoine's disease," which has been applied by some commercial growers in this country to the root-gall or root-knot. It is not only discourteous in the extreme to one who has furnished the world with peonies yet to be excelled by any of us, but it is so unfairly incorrect in its implication as to be ridiculous.

The first observations of this disease of which we have any record were made by Berkeley in 1855 in England. It was next remarked by Greef in Germany in 1864. Since then it has been found in Italy, Austria, Holland, France, Sweden, and Russia. It is not confined to Europe but flourishes in Africa, Asia, India, China, and Japan. Even Australia is not exempt. The disease is pretty well distributed throughout the United States. It is extremely prevalent in the Southern states, and may be found as far West as California.

This malady afflicts many plants. At least two hundred and thirty-five species and subspecies have been found to be susceptible, although not every individual in any species necessarily becomes a victim. Most of the garden plants and many field crops are subject to it.[1] Neither M. Lemoine,

---

1. See *Root-Knot and Its Control*, by Bessey.

nor France, nor yet the peony itself can be held responsible as the originator or sole disseminator of this trouble.

Doubtless the expression arose through ignorance and thoughtlessness, as so many mistakes do. But that does not render it any the less absurd. It would be quite as correct to call root-rot "————'s disease" or "————'s disease," filling in the blanks with the names of any nursery from which you ever received a root touched with rot. From time to time I have imported stock from the house of Lemoine. It has never been anything but entirely clean and healthy. I cannot say as much for stock I have received from some of the nurseries in this country. With the information now accessible to horticulturists who really want it, the time would seem to be here for the name—and the incorrect notion which prompted it—to be dropped into the vasty deep of oblivion.

There is no doubt that both root-gall and botrytis in its various forms are taking toll of the peonies in our gardens. But I think that if gardeners will give their peonies one quarter of the observation and care that they lavish upon other flowers, the exact troubles can be found and successfully combated. Lovers of the rose devote endless hours to the study and cure of its ailments, because it is frankly admitted that—even with all its perfection of beauty—the rose does have some diseases. The peony is at present suffering from its own reputation for hardiness. There is temptation to neglect a flower so cheerful and enduring. In the little garden with mixed planting, crowded beds and overfertilized soil, the peony is more easily the victim of its enemies. It should be watched. Even Achilles had his heel!

"Peonies in the Little Garden": as I read the title of this book once more before I lay down my pen, I have a vision.

I see a little girl leaning upon the seat of an immense old chair covered with needlework. With caressing fingers she traces out the old-fashioned flowers there shown in heaped-up richness. Stately white lilies and cabbage-y roses, imposing crown-imperials and lilacs in purple and mauve, blue irises and dazzling poppies, all receive her absorbed attention. As her gaze falls upon a very fat and very pink peony, the little girl catches her breath. "Some day, when I am a grown-up," she promises herself, "I will have a little garden full of all those flowers. It will be Heaven."

The little girl is now a grown-up. Travel, change, a fair share of life's joys and vicissitudes have been hers. But true to her childish resolve, she has a garden "full of all those flowers." Nor is she disappointed. For it is Heaven.

Appendices

APPENDIX A

References to Articles on the Peony and to Books on Subjects Connected with the Peony

T he names of a few articles on the peony and a few books on collateral subjects are given below. This list is not intended to be complete, but is merely a starting point for anyone who wishes to pursue further the study of the peony in all its branches.

THE PEONY

Anderson, George. "Monograph of the Genus Pæonia." *Transactions Linnæan Society,* 1817.

Baker, J. G. "Monograph of the Genus Pæonia." *Gardener's Chronicle* (1884), Vol. 21 N. S., pp. 732, 779, 780, 828, Vol. 22 N. S., pp. 9, 10.

Correvon, H. "Monograph of Herbaceous Peonies." *The Garden* (1894), Vol. 46, p. 104.

Davis, K. C. "Pæonia." *Cyclopedia of American Horticulture,* Vol. 3, p. 243. Macmillan Company, 1916.

Index Kewensis and references therein.

Four Bulletins published by Cornell University (Agricultural Experiment Station):

Coit, J. Eliot. "The Peony Check-List." *Bulletin of the Cornell University Agricultural Experiment Station* (1907).

Coit, J. Eliot. "The Peony." *Bulletin of the Cornell University Agricultural Experiment Station* No. 259 (1908).

Batchelor, Leon D. "Classification of the Peony." *Bulletin of the Cornell University Agricultural Experiment Station* No. 278 (1910).

Batchelor, Leon D. "Classification of the Peony." *Bulletin of the Cornell University Agricultural Experiment Station* No. 306 (1911).

THE SOIL

Darwin, Charles. *Vegetable Mould and Earth Worms.* D. Appleton & Co., 1900.

King, F. H. *Soil Management.* Orange Judd Co., 1914.

Vivian, Alfred. *First Principles of Soil Fertility.* Orange Judd Co., 1913.

PLANT BREEDING

Bailey, L. H. and A. W. Gilbert. *Plant Breeding.* Macmillan Company, 1915.

Coulter, John M. *Fundamentals of Plant Breeding.* D. Appleton & Co., 1914.

Darbishire, A. D. *Breeding and the Mendelian Discovery.* Cassell & Co., 1913.

Darwin, Charles. *The Effects of Cross and Self Fertilisation in the Vegetable Kingdom,* 1876.

de Vries, Hugo. *Plant Breeding.* Chicago: Open Court Publishing Co, 1907.

THE PEONY IN CHINA AND JAPAN

Bushell, Stephen W. *Oriental Ceramic Art.* D. Appleton & Co., 1899.

Bushell, Stephen W. *Chinese Art.* Victoria and Albert Museum, 1909.

du Cain, Ella. *The Flowers and Gardens of Japan.* A. and C. Black.

Condon, Josiah. *Landscape Gardening in Japan.* Kelly & Walsh, Ltd., 1893.

Gulland, W. G. *Chinese Porcelain.* Chapman & Hall, 1902.

Hobson, Robert L. *Chinese Pottery and Porcelain.* Funk & Wagnalls, 1915.

Smith, R. G. *Ancient Tales and Folklore of Japan.* A. and C. Black, 1908.

Tredwell, W. R. *Chinese Art Motive Interpretation.* Putnam & Sons, 1915.

MISCELLANEOUS

Bose, Jagadis Chunder. "Plant Autographs and Their Revelations." *Smithsonian Institution Publications* No. 2339, 1915. (Contains a most interesting account of recent investigations in plant growth.)

Lipman, J. G. *Bacteria in Relation to Country Life.* Macmillan Company, 1909.

Additional References

A selection of Peony literature subsequent to the publication of Alice Harding's *The Peony* in 1917 and *Peonies in the Little Garden* in 1923.

Boyd, James, editor. *Peonies*. American Peony Society, 1928.

Handbook of the Peony. American Peony Society, 1991 (Revised).

Kessenich, Greta M., editor. *American Peony Society 75 Years.* American Peony Society, 1973.

Kessenich, Greta M., editor. *Peonies: Favorites of Greek Gods and Chinese Emperors.* American Peony Society, 1976.

Kessenich, Greta M., editor. *Peonies 1976–1986.* American Peony Society, 1986.

Kessenich, Greta M. and Don Hollingsworth, editors. *The American Hybrid Peony.* American Peony Society, 1990.

Nehrling, Arno and Irene Nehrling. *Peonies, Outdoors and In.* New York: Hearthside Press, 1960.

Stearn, William T. and Peter H. Davis. *Peonies of Greece.* Kifissia, Greece: Goulandris Natural History Museum, 1984.

Wister, John C., editor. *The Peonies.* Washington, D.C.: American Horticultural Society, 1962.

Short List of Modern *lactiflora* Herbaceous Peonies

SIXTEEN FINE WHITE PEONIES

Bowl of Cream
Bridal Icing (PLATE 7)
Cheddar Charm (PLATE 8)
Cheddar Cheese
Cheddar Regal
Elsa Sass
Festive Powder Puff
Florence Nicholls

Honey Gold
Ivory Jewell (PLATE 12)
Lanchaster Imp
Marshmallow Puff
Miss America
Mothers Choice
Snow Swan
White Ivory (PLATE 25)

EIGHTEEN FINE CREAM TO PALE PINK PEONIES

Angel Cheeks (PLATE 6)
Chiffon Parfait (PLATE 9)
Dawn Pink
Do Tell
Fairy's Petticoat
Golly
Hermione
Moon Over Barrington
Moon River (PLATE 16)

Moonstone
Mrs. F. D. Roosevelt
Nick Shaylor
Norma Volz
Pillow Talk (PLATE 18)
Pink Lemonade (PLATE 20)
Pink Parasol Surprise
Raspberry Sundae (PLATE 22)
Top Brass

FOURTEEN FINE MID TO DEEP PINK PEONIES

Barrington Belle
Bev
Cora Stubbs
Dinner Plate
Emma Klehm
First Lady
Glory Hallelujah

Nice Gal
Pink Jazz
Pink Parfait
Pink Princess
Princess Margaret
The Fawn
Vivid Rose

TWELVE FINE RED PEONIES

Best Man	Karen Gray
Bonanza	Lowell Thomas
Commanche	Maestro
Felix Supreme	Nellie Saylor
Hoosierland	Raspberry Ice
Kansas	Tom Eckhardt

TWELVE FINE FRAGRANT PEONIES

A La Mode (PLATE 1)	Moon River (PLATE 16)
Angel Cheeks (PLATE 6)	Pink Lemonade (PLATE 20)
Cheddar Gold	Raspberry Sundae (PLATE 22)
Dinner Plate	Susie Q
Fairy's Petticoat	Sweet 16
Honey Gold	Vivid Rose

TWELVE PEONIES IDEAL FOR CUTTING AND BRINGING INTO YOUR HOME

Bridal Icing (PLATE 7)	Moonstone
Chiffon Parfait (PLATE 9)	Mrs. Livingston Farrand
Cora Stubbs	Norma Volz
Florence Nicholls	Pillow Talk (PLATE 18)
Hermione	Raspberry Ice
Mister Ed	Top Brass

Short List of Modern Herbaceous Hybrid Peonies

TWENTY FINE RED AND SCARLET HYBRID PEONIES

America (PLATE 5)

Blaze

Buckeye Belle

Burma Midnight

Burma Ruby

Cardinal's Robe

Commando

Dad

Diana Parks

Fire Belle

Heritage

Montezuma

Ole Faithful

Postilion

Raspberry Charm

Red Charm

Red Grace (PLATE 2)

Red Red Rose

Scarlet O'Hara

Walter Mains

FOURTEEN FINE PINK AND SALMON HYBRID PEONIES

Ann Berry Cousins

Brightness

Cytherea

Ellen Cowley

Etched Salmon

Eventide

Flame

Lovely Rose

Ludovica

Paula Fay

Salmon Chiffon (PLATE 23)

Salmon Dream

Salmon Glory

Vivid Glow

SIX FINE TRULY CORAL HYBRID PEONIES

Coral Charm (PLATES 4, 11)

Coral 'n Gold

Coral Sunset

Coral Supreme

Coral Tide

Pink Hawaiian Coral (PLATE 19)

EIGHT FINE WHITE, CREAM, BUFF AND LIGHT YELLOW HYBRID PEONIES

Athena

Claire de Lune

Cream Delight

Garden Peace

Ivory White Saucer

Moonrise

Prairie Moon (PLATE 21)

Sunny Boy

Short List of Modern Tree Peony Varieties

FOURTEEN FINE MOUTAN VARIETIES OF JAPANESE ORIGIN

Godaishu	Renkaku
Hana Kisoi	Shimane Chojuraka
Hinode Sekai	Shimane Otome Mai
Horokumon	Shintenchi
Kamada Fuji (PLATE 13)	Taiyo
Kamada Nishiki	Teni
Kokumon	Yachiyo Tsubaki

SIX FINE MOUTAN VARIETIES DEVELOPED BY WILLIAM GRATWICK

Companion of Serenity (PLATE 10)	Lilith
Ezra Pound	Murad of Hersey Bar
Guardian of the Monastery	Red Rascal

TWENTY-FOUR FINE SAUNDERS HYBRID TREE PEONY VARIETIES

Age of Gold	High Noon
Alhambra (PLATE 3)	Marchioness (PLATE 15)
Banquet	Mystery
Black Pirate	Orion
Canary	Phoenix
Chinese Dragon	Renown
Coronal	Right Royal
Gold Finch	Savage Splendor
Golden Bowl	Spring Carnival (PLATE 24)
Golden Vanitie	Summer Music
Harvest	Thunderbolt
Hesperus	Vesuvain

TWENTY FINE NASSOS DAPHNIS TREE PEONY HYBRIDS

Ariadne   Marie Laurencin

Artemis   Nike

Boreas   Persephone (PLATE 17)

Demetra   Pluto

Gauguin   Redon

Helios   Terpsichore

Hephaestus   Tessera

Icarus   Themis

Iphigenia   Tria

Leda (PLATE 14)   Zephyrus (PLATE 26)

Short List of Modern Itoh Hybrid Peonies

SIX FINE ITOH HYBRID PEONIES

Bartzella

Border Charm

Garden Treasure

Yellow Crown

Yellow Emperor

Yellow Heaven

Peony Varieties Awarded Gold Medal by the American Peony Society Since 1956

1956 Red Charm
1956 Miss America
1957 Kansas
1959 Moonstone
1971 Miss America
1972 Nick Shaylor
1973 Age of Gold (Tree Peony)
1974 Walter Mains
1975 Bu Te
1981 Cytherea
1981 Bowl of Cream
1982 Westerner
1983 Chinese Dragon (Tree Peony)
1984 Dolorodell
1985 Burma Ruby
1986 Coral Charm (PLATES 4, 11)
1987 Norma Volz
1988 Paula Fay
1989 High Noon (Tree Peony)
1990 Sea Shell
1991 White Cap
1992 America (PLATE 5)

The American Peony Society

In 1903, interested peony growers decided to form a special plant society to increase general interest in and knowledge of the cultivation and display of the peony. Other objectives incorporated at the time, still observed today, are

to stimulate the growth and introduction of improved seedlings and crosses of the peony;

to properly supervise the nomenclature of the different kinds and varieties of peonies;

to bring about a more thorough understanding between those interested in its culture;

to increase the peony's use as a decorative flower.

Annual National Peony Flower Exhibitions sponsored by the American Peony Society are held in various parts of the United States every June, where top growers and advanced gardeners compete and show their best blooms. These important shows display the wide range of new varieties available today and are a unique way to see almost the entire peony flower kingdom in one weekend. Some of the more knowledgable and vitally interested peony experts attend and are available for enthusiastic conversations on peony culture.

Informative quarterly bulletins are published by the Society in March, June, September and December. These bulletins contain articles on peony culture and varieties, notes from members, show results and a general wide range of useful peony information. Most of the pieces are written by members of the society, assuring keen interest and contemporary thinking.

The most important function of the American Peony Society is to provide a forum for mutually interested peony lovers to meet, share experiences and trade information and ideas.

American Peony Society
Greta M. Kessenich, Secretary
250 Interlachen Road
Hopkins, Minnesota 55343

Mail Order Sources for Peonies

A & D Nursery
6808 180th S.E.
Snohomish, Washington 98290
U.S.A.

David Austin Roses
Bowling Green Lane
Albrighton
Wolverhampton WV7 3HB
United Kingdom

Caprice Farm Nursery
15425 S.W. Pleasant Hill Road
Sherwood, Oregon 97140
U.S.A.

Craigmore Farming Co. Ltd.
Craigmore, R.D. 2
Timaru, New Zealand

Friesland Staudengarten
D-2942 Jever
Germany

Don Hollingsworth
5831 N. Colrain Avenue
Kansas City, Missouri 64151
U.S.A.

Kelways Nursery
Langport
Somerset TA10 9EZ
United Kingdom

Klehm Nursery
Route 5, Box 197, Penny Road
South Barrington, Illinois 60010
U.S.A.

Heinz Klose
3503 Lohfelden 1
Rosenstrasse 10
Frankfurt, Germany

F. G. Langley
Box 745
Nubeena, Tasmania 7184
Australia

Marsal Pæonies
Old South Road
Dunsandel, R.D.
Canterbury, New Zealand

The New Peony Farm
Box 6105
St. Paul, Minnesota 55118
U.S.A.

Omeo Peonies
6 Hawley Road, R.D. 1
Alexandra, New Zealand

The Peony Gardens
Lake Hayes, R.D. 2
Queenstown
New Zealand

Reath Nursery
County Road 577
Vulcan, Michigan 49892
U.S.A.

Michel Rivière
Pivoines, "La Plaine"
26400 Crest
France

André Viette Farm & Nursery
Route 1, Box 16
Fisherville, Virginia 22939
U.S.A.

Waitawa Orchard
Timaru, R.D. 4
South Canterbury
New Zealand

Wayside Gardens
1 Garden Lane
Hodges, South Carolina 29695
U.S.A.

White Flower Farm
Litchfield, Connecticut 06759
U.S.A.

The Hardy Plant Society Pæony Group
℅ Mrs Pam Adams
Little Orchard
Great Comberton
Nr. Pershore
Worcestershire WR10 3DP
United Kingdom

Herbaceous Peony Disease and Pest Update

P eony diseases have not changed since Alice Harding's time and her commonsense garden sanitation principles remain valid, yet advances have been made in chemical treatment results. Control of the diseases and pests that attack herbaceous peonies has always been a major concern. The disease and pest problems that pose the greatest concern for gardeners are

> *Botrytis cinerea* (gray mold)
> *Cladosporium paeoniae* (leaf blotch)
> Peony rootknot nematode

The control of *Botrytis cinerea* and *Cladosporium paeoniae* are essentially the same, as both of these organisms have a similar life cycle. The organisms that cause gray mold and leaf blotch are favored by wet conditions, and if peonies are planted in sunny locations with good air movement the foliage will dry off fast enough not to allow penetration of spores of the causal fungi. In addition, all top-growth materials should be removed in the fall and composted or destroyed. Usually, if a good composting procedure is used enough heat is produced to result in the destruction of plant pathogenic fungi. If severe outbreaks of these two diseases have occurred in the past or are anticipated, chemicals must be used and three sprayings of recommended fungicides during the growing season are necessary.

The first spray should be done in the spring during the early growth of the peonies. This coincides with the time the plants are most vulnerable and the disease is active. This spraying helps the plants' own defense system fight off infection from any inoculum that may have overwintered in the garden or blown into the garden from adjoining property. The first spray should be done when the spear-like new shoots have emerged from the ground but before any new leaves have unfolded. This spray will also arrest active infections in those shoots which may have had tissue damaged by a late frost. To be effective, the spray should remain on the plant

for at least twenty-four hours before a significant rain.

The second spray is applied ten to fourteen days after the first. This spraying should catch the leaves as they are unfolding as well as any late-appearing ground shoots. A phenological indication of the best time for this spray is when the wood violets are just beginning to bloom.

The third spray is then applied ten to fourteen days after the second, right before or just when the earliest varieties (such as Early Scout) begin to bloom. A chemical recommendation for these three sprayings is Captan (50% wettable powder, also called Orthocide). Full label-recommended rates are applied for the first spraying, half of this recommended rate for the second spraying and also half the rate for the third spraying. If the season has been excessively rainy, use the full recommended rate for the third spraying as this type of weather favors fungus growth.

Always remember to follow the label recommendations, use accurate application equipment, avoid having the chemical solutions touch your skin and clean all equipment thoroughly after use. Garden chemicals should be kept away from children and animals. Caution and common sense should always be practiced when spraying in one's garden.

Garden peony plants infected with peony rootknot nematode are best destroyed, unless the infection is so minor that the plant's performance is not affected. New plants should always be purchased from reliable sources as these growers take great care to sell only clean, nematode-free rootstock. Once a particular garden area has rootknot nematodes, new peony plants should not be planted immediately into this area without a soil exchange. Breaking the nematode's life cycle may also be possible by leaving the area fallow for three to four years, or by raising another type of plant which the nematodes do not affect. It is documented that annual marigolds are a good natural nematode enemy and will help to clean the soil.

One very effective control for rootknot nematode is to maintain a planting site that is high in organic matter. This will promote growth of new root tissue even though some of the older root tissue is destroyed by the nematode. In addition, nematodes are attacked by various fungi that are found in higher populations in soils with higher organic matter.

Tree peonies seem to be relatively free of major disease and pest problems. Although some minor leaf problems may occur from time to time, a single cultural practice can keep plants healthy and vigorous. In early spring, when one can easily examine the plant's branching structure, prune to thin out all the extra internal minor branches. This allows better air circulation within the base and center of the plant and directs the

plant's available stored energy into its main flower-producing shoots. This cultural pruning should begin when the plants are five to six years old and be continued as the plants attain maturity.

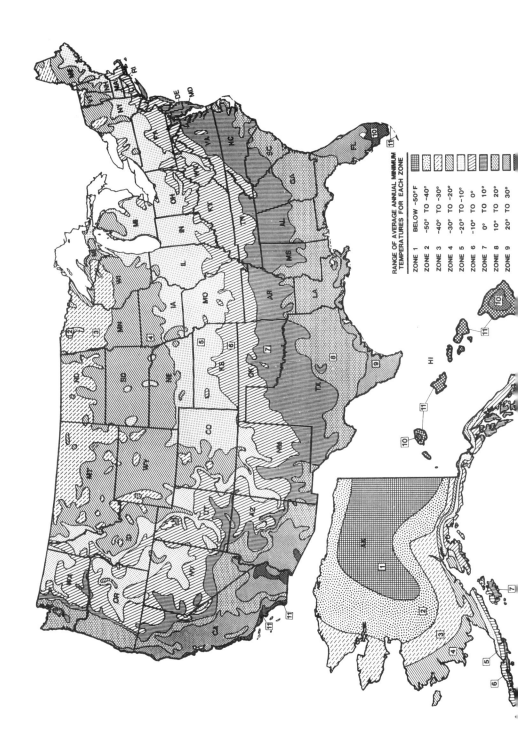

RANGE OF AVERAGE ANNUAL MINIMUM
TEMPERATURES FOR EACH ZONE

ZONE 1   BELOW -50°F
ZONE 2   -50° TO -40°
ZONE 3   -40° TO -30°
ZONE 4   -30° TO -20°
ZONE 5   -20° TO -10°
ZONE 6   -10° TO 0°
ZONE 7   0° TO 10°
ZONE 8   10° TO 20°
ZONE 9   20° TO 30°

Notes and Comments About Peonies and the USDA Zone Map (Revised in 1990)

Herbaceous peonies thrive in USDA plant zones 2 through 7. Success in zone 8 depends on the amount of winter cold to which the plants are normally exposed. Increased altitude helps as elevation generally provides more winter cold effect. As a rule, successful herbaceous peony culture requires approximately 600 winter-hours of temperatures below 32°F. This fulfills the peony plants' dormancy requirements and triggers the plants' inner clock mechanisms to respond properly to the upcoming spring. It is helpful in zone 8 to plant only the early blooming, minimum petaled varieties and then to plant them at ground level or only one inch deep with the topmost crown eye one inch below ground surface. Pine needle mulch is also recommended along with some summer shade and deep waterings to help the plants overcome the intense heat of this plant zone.

Woody tree peonies are recommended for USDA plant zones 3 or 4 through 8. Cultural care must be given in the colder climates to mulching newly planted tree peonies until they establish good root systems. In severe winters, tree peony stems may die above the snow line, but buds beneath the snow or underground should easily regenerate this lost growth during the subsequent season.

Partial spring and summer shade for the warmer plant zones is important, especially during the tree peony's bloom season. Flowers will last longer and be more beautiful if they are shaded during the sunniest part of the day. Deep water tree peonies during hot, and prolonged, summer dry spells.

Index of Peony Cultivated Varieties

PLATE 4. Coral Charm

PLATE 3. Alhambra

PLATE 2. Red Grace

The Peony

PLATE 1. A La Mode